RESELL
RIGHTS PROFITS

How to pull money
from any resell rights product -
even if it's old, out of date,
and everyone owns it!

Resell Rights Profits
Leigh Burke

Design and Layout
Rusdi Saleh

To all those in the arena, whose faces are marred by dust and sweat and blood, who strive valiantly, who err and come up short again and again, because there is no effort without error or shortcoming, but who know the great enthusiasms, the great devotions, who spend themselves for a worthy cause; who, at the best, know, in the end, the triumph of high achievement, and who, at the worst, if they fail, at least they fail while daring greatly, so that their place shall never be with those cold and timid souls who knew neither victory nor defeat.

Other Books and Products by Leigh Burke:

Niche Internet Marketing
http://www.NicheInternetMarketing.com

Niche Internet Marketing - 365 Tips
http://www.NicheInternetMarketing.com/365-Tips

Niche Internet Marketing Videos
http://www.NicheInternetMarketingVideos.com

Wordpress Membership Site
http://www.WPmemberSite.com

Resell Rights Profits
http://www.Resell-Rights-Profits.com

Press Release Software
http://www.Press-Release-Software.com

Instant Testimonials
http://www.Instant-Testimonials.com

Internet Millionaire Videos
http://www.InternetMillionaireVideos.com

Magazine Template
http://www.Magazine-Template.com

Book Template
http://www.Book-Template.com

Website Marketing Magazine
http://www.WebsiteMarketingMagazine.com

Website Marketing Newsletter
http://www.WebsiteMarketingNewsletter.com

Contents

Content

Content

.

Introduction

Thank you for investing in this book and for your time. You made a wise choice and not because I know that it works but because now you will finally make money from your resell rights products even if you have never before.

Sounds like a wild claim doesn't it? Making money from any resell rights product even if it's old, over exposed and everyone already owns it. I know it sounds cheeky but it's true.

Just because people may already own what you have and if they're digital resell rights products the chance is high that they probably do, that's ok. You're going to learn how to pluck your lame old resell product from obscurity and make it a star. Just because your resell product has let itself go over the years doesn't mean that it can't be made sexy again and new life breathed into it extreme make over style.

To launch your sales through the roof this time you need to be different from all the others selling the same thing. This is why most resellers fail because they do what everyone else does and why the more experienced resellers are snapping up your share of the sales because they know this.

To set yourself apart and to sell any resell rights product in your collection no matter how old it is or even if everyone already owns it you must re-create it, don't worry I'll walk you through it every step of the way so that by the time you're finished you'll be snapping up your share of the sales yourself.

So if you're new to resell rights products and aren't quite sure what to do, or if you've never had much luck with them or if you've even been too overwhelmed with the overload of information flung at you from every direction that you've been too stunned to take any action at all, then this is most definitely for you.

You've got the whole package at your fingertips here. By the end of this you'll be a resell rights expert and there won't be anything you won't be able to revive and make money from.

So if you have ever been disheartened or have fallen out of love with resell rights products in the past, thank you for giving it another try because they really can be wildly profitable you just have to know how to do it right, we'll cover all that together.

One other thing, I hope you don't mind that I write like I talk just as if you and I were sitting in a café chatting over a muffin, it's more personal that way and my words flow better when I write in a conversational tone.

So, let's get started.

Leigh Burke

Why I Love Resell Rights Products

Resell rights products or PLR (Private Label Rights) are fantastic because it's the quickest way that I know of to profit from products without having to create them yourself from scratch which means that you can be up and profiting in little time.

So if you have no prior experience in creating your own products this is by far the best way to fast track your product creation in a fraction of the time because the most difficult part has already been taken care of for you.

Look over your collection of resell rights products. The information you have collected cost thousands to create. You probably have in your resell rights arsenal, membership site scripts, software, information products, articles, recipes, graphics, templates and lots more.

The authors who created these products spent significant time and money developing these products for their customers and it's just unfortunate that some resellers devalued it along the way by selling it for well under it's true market value. That's how the 0.99 cent eBay digital products came to be.

This is why in essence instant digital delivery products were banned from eBay in March of 2008 because it was these very 0.99 cent information products that were being constantly recycled and resold that clogged up the eBay marketplace affecting the quality experience of eBay shoppers.

Most resellers used eBay as a means to quickly inflate their feedback rating, to grow their email lists or to sell a higher priced back end product. It worked great for a while until eBay decided to pull the plug on the sale of these digital downloadable products.

The announcement shook the reseller world especially to those who used eBay as their primary source of promotion. Most information resellers were instantly put out of business literally overnight but the clever ones adapted quickly and saw fresh opportunities to dominate a new playing field and flourished with less competition.

Now if you want to sell products on eBay in the US it must be in physical form. It doesn't cost much to burn something to CD or DVD and you have the added advantage of being able to include up sells for more expensive products. The upside to selling physical products is that they have a higher perceived value than their digital counterparts and refund rates tend to be less for physical products. So, positive things came out of the change.

Don't let the fact that the information you purchased went to Timbuktu and back convince you it has no worth because information is always valuable. You just need to build on it to make it hot again.

Not All Private Label Right's Are Created Equal

Before we begin, let's start with the basics. You are only limited by the kind of resell rights you have ownership of. It pays to check your resell rights before you use them as this will ultimately determine what you can do with the content.

The reason behind having private label rights restrictions and why not every author allows the original piece of work to be promoted anywhere or to be sold under a set price is so that the content maintains its integrity for longer and everyone benefits.

How many times have you come across reseller sites and the same product you just paid $47 for is selling for $1? It makes it more difficult for others to sell the same product for more when customers can get it much cheaper elsewhere.

Even though the product is still relevant and is of high quality, due to its pricing loses its perception of value.

When being offered the $1 product compared with its true market value of $47 especially if it's supposed to be a quality product you begin to question the price. What's wrong with it?, if it's being sold at that price then it must be rubbish. This couldn't be further from the truth in fact I have bought some incredible $1 products that were sold way under their recommended value.

So this is why authors stipulate certain restrictions over their work to protect the product's quality and profitability for everyone for as long as possible.

Know Your Rights

Personal Use

No resell rights. This means that the product is for your own personal use and that under no circumstances are you allowed to resell it.

Giveaway Rights

Give Away Rights entitles you to pass on a product free of charge and cannot be sold or the resell rights passed on. The purpose of giveaway rights is usually twofold:

1. It allows the author of the to gain some free viral exposure through other people's giveaway efforts
2. Although the person giving away the product cannot sell it, it at least allows them to give something free and of value to their customers. This could be a great opportunity to use the product as an incentive for people to join their newsletter list.

Rebranding Rights

With these types of rights you are not permitted to alter the content in any way however the author allows you to rebrand (usually with some type of rebranding software provided with the product) the affiliate links within the product with your own.

You are not allowed to sell the rights but you can make money from the sales generated through your rebranded affiliate links.

The upshot for the author is that even though they forfeit the money from their affiliate links because they now go to you through your rebranded affiliate links, they still gain exposure to their website by having their business details in the product go viral. It's a beautiful relationship for both sides, the person giving away the gets to make some money without having had to create a product and the author gains some free exposure without having had to pay a cent for it, win-win.

Basic Resell Rights

These are the weakest of the rights. You only have the right to sell to your products to your immediate customer but they cannot in turn sell that product on to theirs. These usually cannot be edited, altered or re-branded. Although the reseller gets to keep 100% of the product sales these form of rights favor mostly the original author where their links go everywhere their products are promoted giving them free viral marketing through the efforts of resellers.

Master Resell Rights

Unlike basic resell rights resellers have the ability to sell on the product and resell rights to their customers where they in turn can sell them to theirs. The business opportunity is usually the most appealing because customers know they can make money from it. In most cases like basic resell rights, the product cannot be edited or altered in any way and must be sold in the form it was purchased in.

Private Label Rights

These are good rights to get hold of. These are more flexible in that you can alter the content and claim yourself as the author. You are not bound by the same terms and conditions as the other resell rights and you're not promoting the original author but yourself.

There however may be some restrictions that come with private label rights and there may be stipulations on how you can and can't use the content, some examples may be:

You may not be able to sell the content on auction sites
You may only give the product for free if sold with a paid product
You must never sell the product below a certain price
You may not give the product away free or offer it on membership sites, etc.

Unrestricted Private Label Rights

These are the best rights you could ever possibly have.

It's the ability to do whatever you want with the content with zero restrictions. Not only can you re-edit and claim yourself as the author but you can also sell the raw source code (which is usually the text in the form of a Word or text document) as is, without editing.

You can also sell the product itself without editing. You are able to give the content away as freebies and bonuses. You are able to sell the content on auction sites and include them on both free and paid membership sites and can sell them for whatever price you wish.

These types of rights usually look like this:

[YES] Can edit and put your name on it as the author
[YES] Can sell the Rights
[YES] Can be used as article content
[YES] Can be used as website content
[YES] Can be used for blog and auto responder content
[YES] Can be repackaged
[YES] Can sell the Master Resell Rights
[YES] Can sell The Private Label Rights
[YES] Can sell for whatever price you wish
[YES] Can sell the source code
[YES] Can sell on auction sites
[YES] Can be given away as bonuses
[YES] Can be repackaged
[YES] Can be offered on both free and paid membership sites

The only down side to products with unrestricted private label rights is that it's only a matter of time before they are floating everywhere online. If you do have products with these types of rights the best thing you can do to avoid the high competition with other resellers selling the same product as you is to completely transform yours into a different product. We'll talk more in depth about that later on.

So having said that, fish through your treasure trove of resell rights goodies and see what you have access to. If you have private label rights or unrestricted private label rights you basically have no limitations.

If on the other hand you have master resell rights you can still do plenty with your products just without altering the content. When it comes to promoting these types of products it requires a little out of the box thinking.

Pinpointing Your Resell Rights Product So That Your Customers Will Think You Read Their Minds and Love You for It

First things first:

"The Answer to The Million Dollar Question."

How to make lots of money – find out what people want and then give it to them! Sounds too simple? it is! This is why 90% of people fail to make money with resell rights simply because they fail to give people what they want.

How do you give people what they want? you have to find out what it is that they want in the first place and that takes a little research.

Trust me, doing research before you jump into anything will ensure that you turn your losing streak around and actually make money this time, so it's worth it. If you're tempted to jump past this part and skip it altogether, please don't, this really is what makes or breaks your sales everything you do right here at this moment.

Here's what you're going to do. You're going to open up your files where you keep your stash of resell rights products and you're going to pick a product from your massive collection.

Is there anything that stands out to you?
Is there any topic or field that you have some knowledge or an interest in?

Do you have resell rights products on:

- Golf
- Crochet
- Knitting
- Weight Loss
- Health and Beauty
- Nutrition
- Gift Wrapping
- Gift Jars
- Gardening
- Fishing
- Horses
- Pet Care
- Chinese Recipes
- Bath and Soaps Recipes
- Deep Fryer recipes
- Amish Cooking

- Slow Cook Recipes
- Baking
- Cookies
- Cheesecake
- Chocolates
- Breastfeeding
- Childcare
- Make More Money From Home
- Writing
- Product Creation
- Articles
- Graphics
- Letters
- How To Make Your Own Website
- Web templates
- Software
- Scripts
- Yoga
- Martial Arts
- Speed Reading
- Quit Smoking
- Anti Stress
- Kids Party Games
- Guitar Lesson
- Hypnosis
- Memory Improvement
- Goal Setting
- Mind Mapping
- Time Management
- Painting

You no doubt have some or even all of these in your resell rights mother load collection.

Ultimately it is easier to write about what you know. If you feel a little intimidated, please don't be. You know more than you think you do. We each have a wealth of knowledge to share that we've accumulated from our own individual experiences throughout our lives.

Even if you have no prior knowledge on any of the topics in your collection then seize this as a great opportunity to expand your horizons and gain knowledge in a new field.

The next place we're going to start after you pick a resell rights product to promote is a little keyword research.

We are, so to speak starting in reverse; we're beginning at the end. Before we begin to transform our resell product we need to know if there will be a market waiting for us on the other side.

Too often you hear about people that have invested time and money into a sure thing that barely even registered a blip on the radar.

Why?, because people simply weren't interested in it. This is where proper research will save you the time and agony of promoting something that won't sell no matter how much time and money you pour into it. This is the mistake most inexperienced resellers make and how the more savvy resellers are scooping up their sales because they know exactly who their market is.

You're going to start thinking like the other 10% of successful resellers. From now on your customers will be lining up for your products all because you did your homework first.

Beginning with an end in mind, ask yourself this:

• What is your niche?, is it golf, fishing, knitting, childcare, cooking, weight loss, health and beauty, work from home, computers?, etc.

• Who will want your product?, parents, the self employed, knitters, marketers, stay at home parents, dieters?, etc.

• How will they find your product? What kinds of words and phrases are they searching on that will ultimately bring them to your product?

• How many times are they searching for your product each month?

• How much competition is there in your market?, for your product? Is this niche profitable?

Who are your competitors?, can you do what they do better?

These are just some of the things that we need to be aware of before we invest any time into re-creating our resell rights product, that way you are increasing the likelihood your product will be successful than to just hope for the best and that begins long before you re-write your first word for your new resell rights product.

To help answer some of these questions here are some free tools that can help you narrow down your research to locate some really great phrases and keywords people are already searching on to find your product.

What I love about keyword research is that you can find the profitability of any niche. Not only can you freshen up any old resell rights product but you can also use these techniques to identify profitable niches that you can create your own brand new products for.

What to Do if the Resell Rights Doesn't Give Permission To Alter The Content

Just remember to check the type of rights you have first to any product before making any alterations to the content.

If you have unrestricted private label rights where the creator stipulates that you can alter the content and claim yourself as the author, then you're away.

If on the other hand you have a product where the content must be sold unaltered then there are a couple of ways to get around this:

1. Create an accompanying report to go along with the product itself. This can be used as a special related bonus targeted to your offer that customers receive upon purchase. That way you can add in any extra information that the ebook may be lacking without violating the rights of the ebook itself. This can be used as a list building tool or to place your affiliate links in for products related to your resell rights product.

2. Another thing you can do without breaching the terms and conditions of the product is to use the information as a guideline for creating your own prod-

uct. Do not under any circumstances copy it that would be plagiarism but use it to get ideas from.

If the product is two years old or more, what information does it lack? What technological developments have taken place since it was first published? What's hot in that niche right now? What's outdated and no longer relevant? Get ideas from it, do your research to answer your questions and then make it even better when you write it from scratch.

Using those two techniques not only makes the product fresh but you also have the added bonus of owning full rights over the content because you yourself created it.

Ok, now you know that you can pretty much work with any resell product you have in your collection no matter the types of rights you have.

Now let's get back to the matter of choosing a product to work with.

Take a look on www.magazines.com to see what's selling. It will give you an indication of what people are interested in. It's a great sign when people are prepared to shell out money for a product usually revealing that there is money to be made in that niche. People will pay money when it comes to their passion.

See if any of the topics match any of your resell rights products from the list of categories.

Just simply click on the "Browse Magazines" tab near the top of the screen. Open up each category and take note any topics of interest that you may want to save for future products. There are lots of categories that are bound to fit in with some of your resell rights products. Everything from Animals & Pets to Business & Finance to Cooking & Food, Crafts, Environmental, Golf, Graphic Arts, Health & Fitness, Hobbies, Parenting and more.

Let's say that you decide to choose "fishing" from your vast collection of resell rights. We begin our research in magazines.com to see if there are any paid magazines related to fishing. We perform a search in the search tool provided.

There are currently 35 paid fishing magazines with prices ranging from 18 issues for $11.95 for the Western Outdoors magazine to 6 issues for $28.95 for the Sporting Classics magazine and every price range in between. This is great; people are paying good money for this kind of information. You'll find that subscribers will range from enthusiasts all the way through to the diehard competitors.

Looking at some of the magazine issues and topics will also help us with our own product research as this is usually spot on the kind of information this market is looking for and again, if they're willing to shell out hard earned dollars, we're on the right track.

Let's dig even deeper by looking at their popularity rank, reviews and comments.

In February 2009 there are currently 1,948 magazines in www.magazines.com.

If we check out the popularity of some of our fishing magazines it can give us even more insight into what people want.

The magazine "Field and Stream" ranks at #44. This is fantastic considering it's 44 out of 1,948. Its ratings ranged from 4/5 to 5/5 stars and the comments were from satisfied customers who enjoyed the information in the articles. One customer was glad he was able to purchase some good lures from their magazine (we'll include that in our own product).

On that note, I uncovered a nice little fishing affiliate program that will pay you up to $40 for each sale. We could add a link for it in our product, not bad for an up sell.

http://www.eveningsecretfishing.com

eBay also has thousands of fishing related products ranging from lures to fishing line, sonar equipment for locating fish, boats, jigs, weigh scales, mugs, mailboxes, games, clothing, waders, posters, fishing rods and a whole heap more. This is one serious niche. You could even build a subscriber list with your product and send out alerts with eBay links to fishing supplies and make some nice additional, ongoing sales. Your customers will appreciate it because it's targeted specifically to them.

Fishing is so popular that it's in the top 10 hottest categories in eBay pulse which further proves we're on to a good thing here:

http://pulse.ebay.com/Sporting-Goods_W0QQsacatZ382

Check out the link to see the volume of fishing products being sold.

http://shop.ebay.com/items/?_nkw=fishing&_sacat=0&_fromfsb=&_trksid=m270.11313&_odkw=fishing+lures&_osacat=0

Let's continue to dig some more and check out what kind of interest fishing cooks up.

Google Trends is a great place to look. Not only will it reveal the traffic activity for our niche but any trends such as seasonality which we can take advantage of.

www.google.com/trends

Looking at Google Trends fishing has an active amount of interest. There also tends to be some seasonality and a great time to get into from about March to July coinciding with the weather which would be the best fishing months. Because we know it's seasonal we know that this niche without fail will be popular predictably at the same time each year which means a nice, predictable income for you.

When your market quiets down during the off peak season, don't forget on the other side of the world, the fishing season is just picking up.

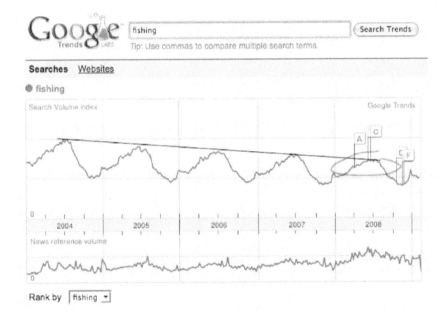

Now let's check out our competition as we Google search the term fishing.

Little tip: if you are not from the US and you want to undertake an accurate Google search but for some reason Google keeps defaulting to your country's settings then you can either clear your cookies or just click on this link which will give you the Google US search bar:

www.google.com/webhp

So, we've searched for fishing in Google and we get:

Results **1 - 10** of about 199,000,000 for **fishing** [definition]. **(0.08 seconds)**

It's important that you use US Google as your country's default one will give you different results, e.g.:

- Google US 199 million pages for fishing
- Google (default to country) 174 million pages for fishing

That's a difference of 25 million pages.

That's a 25 million/199 million = 12.5% difference, so for the purpose of accuracy use Google US if you're from another country rather than the Google search feature that defaults to your country's version.

Now Back To Our Results.

Whoa! There are currently nearly 200 million pages related to fishing!

That's way too much competition and it would be difficult for your customers to find you floating in that vast sea of pages. It would be difficult to rank on the first few pages of Google due to the sheer number of competing pages and that's all the pages with the term "fishing" in them.

We know fishing is a lucrative niche because there are lots of Adwords ads on the right hand side of the page. People are actually paying to promote fishing related products so there is money to be made.

Let's look at the competition to see if we can outrank them.

On the first page in the number one spot we have Wikipedia, would be next to impossible to outrank them because they are a popular authority site with tonnes of sites linking to them, lots of traffic and plenty of user participation which allows it to consistently maintain its high rankings.

The second spot is www.fishing.com, which surprisingly has lots of links within its site but not much content. I was expecting to see some heavy duty content keeping people coming back for more. It has lots of Adsense at the top of the page and on the right hand side.

Now here's an interesting point, they have a big pink banner advertising classified ads. With their rankings you could place a classified ad on their site. With time and sales made you could even approach the owner of this site and negotiate to place your own banner on their site for a monthly fee. Try going for one month as a test. If it pulls in twice or three times or more than what you paid you've landed a winner (no pun intended).

Just looking at www.fishing.com and all of the Adsense and classified ads they promote on their site, I'm sure they would be open to your proposal.

After performing a little more investigative research on http://www.networksolutions.com/whois/index.jsp we find that the site was created back in 1996. Google places higher importance on older sites that rise naturally over time in the search engines. The older a site and the more sites linking to it, the higher the ranking it assigns it and the more solid its position in the search engines.

Their site only has a page rank of 5 which is quite surprising. Page rank can vary from the lowest being 0 (a brand new site) to the highest being 10 (www.cnn.com) so www.fishing.com's page rank is ok, I thought it would have been higher considering their number 2 position. Perhaps if you have tonnes of inbound links from authority sites with high page rank you might be able to rank on the first page too, hey you never know.

You can calculate a site's page rank using by going here:

http://www.calculatepagerank.com

In terms of our competition the best thing to do in our case is to find a part of the fishing niche with low enough competition that we can dominate.

With 100,000 other web pages or less we should be able to snap up multiple spots on the first page of Google for several keyword search terms driving lots of that lovely traffic to our site as opposed to fighting tooth and nail to claw our way onto the first page with nearly 200 million other fishing related pages.

Recap: Ok, so fishing is a very lucrative niche judging by:

1. The Adwords ads on the right hand side of the screen in the search results. Only advertisers making money on a consistent basis would pay to promote a product on Adwords. Keep doing a Google search for your keywords at least twice a week. If the same ads keep showing up then that's a strong indicator they're making money because they can afford to maintain their position.

2. People are paying perfectly good money for fishing related magazines so that means that they would pay for your product.

3. Fishing related affiliate programs (in www.Clickbank.com too) as well as fishing products on eBay. These products wouldn't be sold if there wasn't a hungry market for it.

4. It's an evergreen market with a good supply of customers.

So far so good.

Let's dig even further so we can identify a smaller but less competitive corner of the market and to find approximately how much of that traffic could be yours for the taking.

So here we go. Click on the Google keyword tool. https://adwords.google.com/select/KeywordToolExternal

Keywords are important because they dictate your product content.

Whatever your keywords are will help shape the direction your product takes as you will see once we narrow down some profitable, low competition keywords.

Ok so we've entered our main keyword of fishing and the Google search tool has returned several keywords. It's our job to weed out the best ones.

I see that bass fishing and salmon fishing look like good contenders with 480 and 720 searches for the month previous. This tells me to dig down even deeper by getting more specific. I decide to do some more keyword research for the different fish types which returned a lot of great results.

This gives me lots of great keywords and keyword combinations so I search even further to determine the amount of daily traffic each keyword group returns.

http://tools.seobook.com/keyword-tools/seobook

In seobook.com I see that bass fishing returns 14,300 Google searches per month (471 per day), this is the approximate number of times people are searching for the phrase bass fishing.

WordTracker	WordTracker count	Google daily est	Yahoo! daily est	MSN daily est	Overall daily est
fishing	2179	2,724	782	340	3,843
ice fishing	435	544	156	68	767
fly fishing	433	541	155	68	764
fishing knots	416	520	149	65	734
bass fishing	377	471	135	59	665
fishing boats	307	384	110	48	541
fishing tackle	203	254	73	32	358
fishing buddy	188	235	67	29	332
fishing games	170	213	61	27	300
fishing lures	158	198	57	25	279
fishing gear	144	180	52	22	254
aluminum fishing boats	135	169	48	21	238
deep sea fishing	129	161	46	20	228
fishing equipment	128	160	46	20	226
fishing pole	125	156	45	20	220
ice fishing equipment	121	151	43	19	213

This is a fantastic amount of traffic and that's just for Google not to mention Yahoo and MSN. Let's look at the number of competing pages for "bass fishing". Note how we use "quotes" so that we can identify our exact number of competing pages for this phrase, this gets rid of any other general pages that have bass fishing with any other words in the title.

Ok, so "bass fishing" returns 4.1 million other competing pages. Remember how we want to get that down to 100,000 or less so that we can dominate those keyword phrases?

Note: A point of interest, 6 out of 10 results on the 1st page of Google for the search term "bass fishing" are videos. Just shows the power and influence of videos on Google and how they can be great tools to rank highly.

Let's create some more long tail, specific phrases to eliminate the amount of competition. The more specific, the more targeted the better the results, for example which would be more likely to convert into a sale?, people searching on the phrase "fishing" or people searching for the phrase "the best fishing lure to catch sea bass"?

People searching for fishing could be looking for the heck of it, looking at fishing tournament results, fishing techniques, fishing equipment, fishing news, fishing videos. It's too broad and you can't be all things to all people. The people you want make up a small part of that general market.

People searching on long tail keywords know what they want and have a specific purpose in mind. They're ready to buy. Those are the people you want.

Looking through SEO book and using the Google suggest feature which gives you alternative keyword suggestions based upon your search you can come up with some pretty decent keywords including some the Google suggestion tool may have missed. Doing keyword research like this allows you to cover every possible angle to unveil all of those little overlooked keywords that are the silent traffic generators with very little competition.

The above techniques are free and work well but another tool that I love to use that helps me to uncover hidden niches even quicker is Micro Niche Finder http://www.micronichefinder.com/

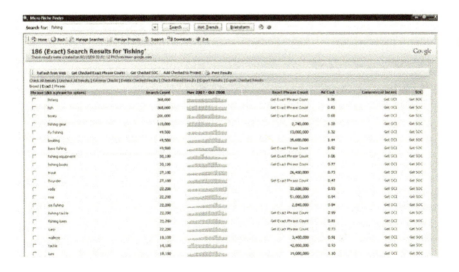

It also uses Google to unearth low competition niches. It determines the amount of competing pages, the profitability by factoring in how much advertisers are paying for Adwords ads and any matching affiliate programs associated with that niche. The added advantage of knowing how much people are paying for Adwords is to identify some profitable keywords and make some nice Adsense earnings for yourself. You make money from your competitors for them to place relevant ads on your site, how's that for awesome?

You learned how to determine this for free and the steps to how we got there which is good to have a working knowledge on how all of the moving parts fit together. Micro Niche Finder just does it quicker.

Here are some keywords Micro Niche Finder came up with.

KEYWORD	SEARCHES	COMPETITION
Cape cod fishing	1,000	17,000
Largemouth bass fishing	1,900	68,000
Bass fishing lures	3,600	59,000
Bass fishing tackle	1,900	48,000
Pompano fish	1,000	4,800
Peacock bass fishing	1,300	61,000
Bass fishing tips	6,600	81,000
Crappie jigs	1,900	26,000
Crappie tackle	220	1,600
Walleye fish	1,300	27,000
Crappie fishing tips	1,300	39,200
Crappie fish	1,300	19,900
Bluegill fishing	1,900	24,600
Crappie bait	590	4,090
How to catch crappie	880	6,100
Catfish bait	5,400	64,000
Fish types	1,300	45,000
Crappie lures	1,300	4,570
Crappie fishing techniques	880	11,000
Pompano fishing	480	4,480
Saltwater fishing lures	880	19,300
Grouper fishing	1,300	38,000
Wahoo fishing	1,000	21,000
Flounder fishing	2,400	41,000
Mullet fishing	590	7,130

Bass fishing techniques	2,400	57,000
Big bass fishing	1,300	25,000
Fishing jigs	1,600	42,000
Lake trout fishing	1,600	51,000
Largemouth bass fishing tips	480	595
Largemouth bass habitat	260	1,500
Winter bass fishing	390	10,700
How to catch redfish	390	1,350
Rainbow trout fishing	720	53,000

Total number of searches per month: 51,360

That's a potential 616,320 searches per year, of course that number will vary especially based upon seasonal fluctuations within the fishing niche but still, that's some serious traffic and that's just scratching the surface. There are lots more searches out there that I haven't even touched upon. This list by no means includes all fish types either.

This is traffic you could be monopolizing for yourself because the competition is at a level that makes it possible to do so. Very powerful.

Imagine setting up your advertising so that you receive this traffic passively 24 hours a day with sales funneling into your account for years to come, long after you promote your product.

You can use your keywords to shape the content for your resell rights product and to create targeted ads, articles and blogs, Squidoo lenses and Hubpages that will literally drive traffic to your offer, but more on that later.

So here we are, re-creating your product from the ground up. We first saw what kind of content people were paying money for. Then we determined that there definitely was money in it judging from the ads from our competitors. Then we further narrowed it down to the types of keywords that had the traffic we wanted and now we finally get to the bottom most layer, the exact questions our future customers are asking, questions we could then answer in our product.

If you want to know the kinds of questions people are asking try forums, http://directory.big-boards.com is a great place to start and in terms of our niche they have 3 forums dedicated to fishing alone.

Searched for: **fishing**

Recreation : Outdoors : **Fishing** (3)

forums matches

Outdoors Best
Fishing and hunting message boards

http://outdoorsbest.zeroforum.com/

... Boating, Hunting and Shooting, from Primedia Outdoors Digital, a division of Primedia, Inc. ...

info · stats

Stripers Online
Striped bass and surf **fishing** community

http://www.stripersonline.com/surftalk...

... **fishing** and surf **fishing** community centered around 30 active forums - regional, how-to and specific **fishing** forums. ...

info · stats

IFish.net
Pacific Northwest **fishing** and hunting forum

http://www.ifish.net/forum/ubbthreads...

info · stats

Hardcore Sledder
Snowmobiles discussion forums

http://www.hardcoresledder.com/forums/

... There are many off-topic forums involving topics such as hunting and **fishing**, digital cameras, current events and even a cooking forum. ...

info · stats

You can also find out important statistics for each forum like membership numbers.

Outdoors Best
Fishing and hunting message boards

http://outdoorsbest.zeroforum.com/

... Boating, Hunting and Shooting, fro

info - stats

keywords: fishing, hunting.

Daily statistics for last month:

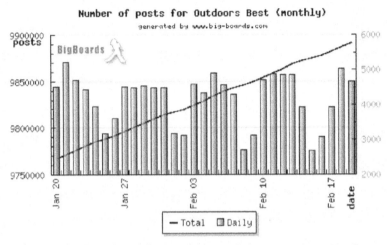

Number of posts for Outdoors Best (monthly)
generated by www.big-boards.com

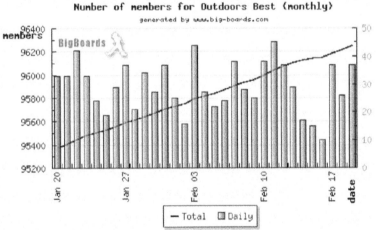

Number of members for Outdoors Best (monthly)
generated by www.big-boards.com

From the top graph we see that there has been anywhere from 2,500 up to 5,500 posts daily from members, this is a very active forum.

The number of members sits around the 96,000 mark. A huge, captive audience with a passion for fishing and hunting that actively participate in that niche.

Let's look at some of the things they talk about.

- What is the best time of day to fish for sturgeon?
- Where are the fish?
- What do I need to catch bass?
- When is the right time to start fishing for bass?
- Where do you get fresh smelt from?

The great thing about big-boards is that you can even promote your product in your signature file when you've finished it. Your highly targeted product is getting directly in front of your target audience.

Yahoo answers is another great site. This is a highly trafficked site where your market is giving huge clues about their interests. It's like getting inside your buyers minds. If you can answer those questions and fulfill a need with your resell product you've got a winner.

http://answers.yahoo.com

Some questions on Yahoo answers targeted to the fishing niche.

Just click on the link above and search for "fishing" using the available search toolbar and questions targeted to your niche will appear. This is great for gathering information for your ebook.

Here are some examples of real questions in the fishing niche that allow you to laser focus your content for real people.

- How do I keep a fish alive when fishing from shore?

- What is the best pike fishing technique?

- What is the best kind of fishing line to use for bass?

- How do you choose a good fishing line?

- When does the bass fishing season start?

- There are endless questions that will give you plenty ideas for content. Check out some of the answers to give you ideas but don't just stop there, do your own research and go into more detail.

Once you start to collect relevant information to update your resell rights product you can start to re-write your content.

Now that we've covered the fundamentals we can move on to revamping your resell rights product from the grass roots up.

Reviving Your PLR Extreme Make Over Style

Ok, now that we've identified our niche, the keywords people are searching on to find our niche, we even know what kinds of questions people are asking within our niche, now it's time to flesh out or research and start creating our product.

The next thing we have to do is our own information gathering. We will begin with the information side first then work our way to the cosmetics last because even though it may be the graphics that gets our product noticed, it will be the content itself that determines the value of the product.

You can start your information gathering by visiting your local magazine shop, book store, library, Google information search, reading articles, blogs and newsletters. This should give you some ideas but don't copy directly from these sources, you can easily create your own content as I will share with you in the coming pages.

All of the research we've done up to this point has allowed us to not only identify a lucrative market but also the terms your market is searching for even down to the types of questions they're asking.

It is this information that will shape the direction of our product because we will include these keywords and questions in our content to make our product up to date and highly relevant.

Looking at our keyword list I would group like categories so that the information is organized and flows well.

Fish types
Crappie fish
How to catch a crappie
    Crappie jigs
    Crappie tackle
    Crappie fishing tips
    Crappie lures
Bass fish
    Bass fishing tips
Bass fishing tackle
Bass fishing lures
Big Bass fishing
Pompano fish
Peacock bass fish
Walleye fish
Bluegill fish

As you can see this is starting to shape into a real product with the guesswork completely removed from the equation. At least you know all of the content is relevant because these are real terms that real people are searching on.

I would then do further research in Yahoo Answers to identify more questions to base your content around. You could even base your chapters around popular questions where your chapter is dedicated to answering that question in more depth.

At this point you have the beginnings of a product in your own right, you can also incorporate your private label rights product into information gathering by using it as a framework to build your new and improved product around.

Gather information answering your researched questions, add information that updates your old resell rights product. What has changed in the fishing industry since the resell rights product was first created? What types of fishing techniques work the best? Are there any new flies or lures available on the market that will catch even more fish that didn't exist at the time the resell rights product was first released?

When re-writing your product I would start with your table of contents, this creates a skeleton for you to work with as well as a natural progression for your content as it flows from point to point.

This is how I always start when creating products. I copy and paste my table of contents directly underneath the original table of contents. This copied version is the one that I alter and add to. What I then do is flesh out my copied table of contents by adding 3 to 4 points for each chapter based upon my research and flesh it out further.

For example (this is just a brief, rough outline of course you're going to have your own ideas and direction this is just to get you started).

Table Of Contents:
• **Introduction**
• **Fish types**
• **Crappie fish**
• **Crappie jigs**
• **Bass fishing tips**
• **Bass fishing tackle**

(copy and paste directly underneath it and start fleshing it out).

Introduction

Does catching the best fish come down to just plain old luck? Why is it that some people are able to catch just about any fish known to man while others go home empty handed with nothing more than tall tales about the one that got away?

I'm glad you found my book because you're about to discover the secret fishing techniques used by the pro's to attract the best fish over and over again without fail. If you couldn't catch anything other than a cold before then get very excited because your losing streak is about to end immediately.

Fish types

There are an estimated 25,000 of species of fish occupying our oceans the world over with 400 of that figure comprised of bass alone making bass such a popular and diverse game fish.

Crappie fish

Crappie fish are very popular for their flavor and are considered to be the most delicious tasting of the fresh water fish making them fantastic game for fishing enthusiasts. Because the crappie fish has such a diverse diet they can be caught in a manner of different ways.

Crappie jigs

These are special lures that seem to magnetize crappie fish, they effectively mimic prey that crappie are drawn to.

Crappie are primarily sight feeders, if they can't see the lure in the water they won't bite, simple as that. The popular theory amongst professional fishermen is that color of chartreuse seems to work best because it stands out regardless of water clarity and conditions.

Bass fishing tips

Being such an abundant fish the bass has over 400 known species within the bass family alone making it a very popular fish.

Bass, especially of the large mouth variety tend to occupy the top 5 to 10 feet of water. This is because this is the warmest layer as it resides closest to the surface with the greatest sun exposure and oxygen levels. So it stands to reason that when targeting these fish you should keep your rig in or around those depths, go too deep and you could miss them. Using soft textured, lighter colors seem to work the best.

Bass fishing tackle

Like the crappie, bass are also primarily sight feeders. Lures that seem to work well for this type of fish are the ones that resemble natural looking grubs. The bass' eyesight is so keen that even your clothing can play a part in your success. Tone down your clothing colors as brighter clothing will only draw attention to yourself especially when making sudden movements which will only end up spooking them.

You see? You're creating your very own product. The more you add to it the more it looks like an ebook. Now all that's left to do is go into more detail for each point and flesh it out even further. Don't forget to add a conclusion with a link to your website or further products or related affiliate programs that run along similar lines as your ebook content to generate even more backend sales.

When re-writing the content try putting it into your own words with your point of view, opinions and perspective. Adding the research you gathered will only make it more your own and transform it into a completely new product.

How To Double Your Writing Speed

Take all of the information gathered, take 5 pages of it and read for 30 minutes. Get on your computer and re-write what you read in your own words with your own thoughts and opinions thrown in.

Don't over think it, just write. Don't edit as you go as this will only disrupt the creative process. Do this for a couple of days and it will become instinct, you'll be churning out content with ease. The words will flow like honey. Go back and edit when you've finished and you'll be amazed at what you wrote while you were in the zone.

Another tip that helps me write faster is that if you have private label rights products that you have permission to alter don't alter the text line by line as it only disrupts your natural thought processes trying to fit into another writers mould. Find your own voice and your own writing style and the words will flow naturally and your own personality will shine through. So take whole paragraphs, read them thoroughly and write them in your own words spliced in with all of the research you've gathered along the way. It will come across as fresh and new and becomes your own unique content in your own right.

There Really Are Several Benefits To Creating Your Own Product Or Recreating A Private Label Rights Product:

1. You set yourself apart as an authority and an expert on your chosen topic
2. Others in your field will want to do business with you and so your business will grow quickly
3. Build trust and confidence with your customers
4. Branding and recognition, once you get your name out there people will begin to buy simply on the strength of your name and reputation
5. You are able to promote your product however you wish because you own full rights to it, you call the shots
6. Use your products to build your business
7. You develop a new and valuable skill in product creation
8. Create a money tree by being able to create products at the drop of a hat, have several money making income streams with each product you have working for you
9. Through firsthand experience being able to mentor and coach others on how to create their own products.
10. Create your own affiliate programs and have an army of affiliates promoting your products for you.

It's great being someone's affiliate but the true money is in creating your own products.

That's ok if you don't like writing because I have some great alternatives for you.

Re-Writing Your Resell Rights Product Hands Free

There is Windows based voice recognition software available now that you can purchase online named Dragon Naturally Speaking.

http://www.nuance.com/

It works in recognition to your voice and pronunciation. You simply talk into your computer using a microphone and it will turn your spoken word into written text. It may take a little time for it to adapt to your voice patterns and accent but when it does its accuracy increases resulting in fewer spelling errors and less editing for you.

http://www.nuance.com/naturallyspeaking/resources/poguevideo.asp

If you own a Mac the Dragon Naturally Speaking equivalent is http://www.macspeech.com it basically does the same thing Dragon Naturally Speaking does (as it uses Nuance's accuracy technology, the same creators behind Dragon Naturally Speaking) only instead for the Mac version.

http://www.youtube.com/watch?v=N1yKEKRU3hE

Here is another voice recognition based software you might want to check out.

www.e-speaking.com

Windows Vista has a voice recognition feature of its own. People have mixed reactions about this tool. They either love it or hate it, if you have Vista and you want to try it out, here's how.

Here's a quick tutorial:

http://www.youtube.com/watch?v=3qWJ-Y3zRF4&feature=related

Completely Hands Off Product Creation

If writing's not your thing at all then there's another solution.

Outsource the task to someone else also known as Ghost Writing where you hire a writer for your project for a fee. They do all of the hard work for you they research and write the entire thing for a negotiated fee while you take the credit as the author and you own the product outright as if you created it yourself.

This is a great option if you can afford it, if not start writing your own content until you can afford to hire a ghost writer. Content creation can be time exhaustive and outsourcing the task to someone else allows you to focus on growing your business.

How much do ghost writers charge? The price will vary according to the size of your project, obviously a 200 page ebook will cost more to produce than a 10 page one. Some ghost writers charge per page, some charge per word.

The going rate for each page varies from $10 to $50 and everything in between. Those that charge per word can ask for 1 cent to 20 cents per word or more. You should be able to get discounts for bigger projects and when working with bulk orders, i.e. more than 1 project at a time.

Ghost writer's fees also depend on the level of expertise they have, the more expertise, positive feedback and testimonials the higher the fee. You basically get what you pay for.

The best way to find a ghost writer is to visit two of my favorite forums, the www.warriorforum.com and www.digitalpointforum.com I've been very fortunate when it comes to locating some top quality writer's on these two forums, you will too and I'll give you a few tips on how to go about it.

First off for the warriorforum.com you will need to join up so that you can post questions. You will not be able to send any private messages to prospective ghost writers until you have made at least 30 posts in the forum first. Register, get in there and contribute. Get involved in discussions. You will find that you know more than you think you do and will learn a lot along the way. Many great businesses were created in this very forum and so it should be treated like "gold" as Allen the warrior forums creator so beautifully put it.

When searching for a ghost writer on the warrior forum the most important thing is to look at any testimonials in their sales copy if they are offering their services as a warrior special offer.

Look at any additional posts and comments that have been left by past clients they have done business with. Do a search for their username and all posts and threads they ever participated in will show up, that way you read comments they've left, feedback good or bad from other members (which will help to make your decision an informed one). Another thing that I look for is how long they have been a member of the forum and their post count.

If they have been there for 6 months or more and have contributed to the forum, have been thanked by people chances are they are the real deal.

If on the other hand they've been a member for only 1 month, have a post count of 30 that was obtained in a couple of days and all of the comments they've left are random one liners that don't make sense or contain any real value, then beware.

That's not to say that all are like that, everyone has to start somewhere and everyone has a low post count to begin with but there are those who will try to make a quick buck, this little bit of intelligence gathering will steer you in the right direction come decision time.

Take home point, the more information the ghost writer leaves, the more contactable and out in the open they are, the more genuine they are because they have nothing to hide.

When your post count is over 30 you can start private messaging potential ghost writers. Try contacting those that have left comments regarding their services, past customers to help you make your decision.

Just let them know that you saw their comment on a thread and are looking at hiring a ghost writer and would they recommend that particular writer. What was the thing about their service that most impressed them? Was their overall experience with that writer good/bad? Always let them know where you found their post so that they don't think you're trying to spam them.

Another hugely important thing is to look at their work samples. Do a search to see if they are listed as a contributing author on www.ezinearticles.com, www.goarticles.com, etc. This also helps you further gauge their content quality and variation of writing styles. Chances are they will be publishing several types of articles and content and seeing their versatility will further help you in your decision making.

The next thing to do is to get in touch with the author and buy just two articles from them to test the waters. This is so that you can judge their turnaround time and content quality for yourself.

Why articles?, because you're not tied into a huge commitment than if you were with say a 10 page mini report or ebook straight out of the gate. That would set you back $150 or more, a huge chunk of change if the job isn't up to scratch. Articles are good to gauge quality without the huge price tag and commitment that comes with bigger projects, start small.

I've had a few instances of hit and miss myself. I did my due diligence, checked their ratings, talked to customers and dove into the waters.

One guy was an amazing writer but never delivered on time, he always forgot and I would have to chase him up. I always got my content in the end and was satisfied with the quality but it always left me feeling a little worried that it would jeopardize my own deadlines as a result.

I decided to keep him as a standby writer but have since looked elsewhere and tested a whole pool of other writers, narrowed it down based upon quality and timeliness and am very happy with the result, granted I pay a little extra but it's absolutely worth it for your business when you get consistency.

Another guy I hired just had a case of bad luck. After a week I still hadn't heard back from him, I followed up and was told he needed a few more days then on the day he was to deliver his computer crashed losing my articles amongst other things. He was good enough to refund my money so I was happy about that. A great lesson to me was to have more than one writer at your disposal because anything can happen.

Another fella was selling articles for $2 a pop. His pitch got my interest so I purchased 10 (do not try this at home!), when I got them back they were terrible. They were fragments of other articles strewn together Frankenstein style. There was no way I was ever going to use them, no amount of grammatical surgery was ever going to save them. So $20 lighter and a whole lot wiser I made sure I thoroughly did my homework first before bulk buying. I got what I paid for.

Back to the purchasing, if you're happy with the turnaround time for your 2 test articles and even more so with the content and price then this is the kind of writer you want to have working with you.

Go ahead and negotiate your project with them. Some require 50% upfront which is reasonable. They will send you updates and progress reports over time so that you can monitor the direction and quality of the project and you can make changes along the way so the end result is something you feel good about and are proud to have your name on.

Subject to availability and work load the typical turnaround time for projects of 30 pages or less is on average 7 to 21 days, this is dependent upon your writer but this I've found seems to be the average turnaround time. Always make sure that you know the approximate turnaround time so that there are no surprises when you are pressed to a deadline yourself.

For www.digitalpointoforum.com pretty much the same due diligence is required. You have the added advantage of an iTrader rating. You can see how long they have been a member and read the comments customers have left. If their iTrader history looks a little checkered with a mixture of good and bad feedback I'd be a little weary of ever using them.

If their iTrader rating is around 10 and over and their history is impeccable with positive ratings then dig a little deeper and ask questions to their past customers. For me I've had great content from a writer with 7 iTrader rating as I have with writers with 88 and 368 iTrader ratings. Ask questions, use your discretion and test the waters before committing to any big projects.

Basically in terms of price, I have never received an article over $10 I didn't like. $18 articles were amazing and this particular writer went over and above the call of duty by infusing her personality into the article and by creating a catchy title. Don't worry you don't have to pay that much because I've also paid for some fantastic $5 and $6 articles too. It's when you get into the $3 and less category that quality seems to be reflected in price and the saying "you get what you pay for" really does apply. You be the judge. You will get a feel for the level of quality out there and what your dollar gets you and you'll develop a nose for weeding out the good from the bad.

Another option if you seriously don't like to write your own content, running along similar lines as Dragon Naturally Speaking you can actually record your audio, save it as an MP3 file and email it to companies that will scribe it into written text for you. The quality of the content is dependent upon the quality of audio you supply them with. The fuzzier and cracklier it is the longer it will take to decipher and transcribe, the more expensive it becomes.

This is a great option if you don't want to type your own content. These companies will remove spelling errors and alter grammar slightly so that it makes sense but that's the extent of their corrective services. You still need to do all the research yourself for your content and word it so that you're happy with the outcome in text form.

You can always alter it later, you receive it in PDF and .txt form.

This service costs less if you allow them to have it longer. Priority projects will cost more by the page. For their 24 hour express service you are looking at $2.50 per minute compared to 0.75 cents per minute if you wait for 3 weeks. It's entirely up to you.

http://castingwords.com/store

Another very good site which charges $30 for 30 minutes worth of transcribed audio which means that you could easily get 15 pages of written text for $30, that's a cool $2 per page, very good deal.

http://www.transcriptionsservice.com/audio.html

Don't think that you have to stick to the written word either. With the advances in technology these days the options are limitless.

You can turn your digital products into physical products and since these have a higher perceived value you can charge more for them.

Making Your Own Physical Products

By simply recording your voice to audio using a microphone and the free software found in this report http://www.streamingaudio4free.com/dlpefa you are able to add the audio to your website or burn it to CD giving you an immediate physical product. The great thing is that the CD only cost pennies but you can charge $19.97 for it. The audio CD is also a great entry level product for more expensive up sells and backend sales.

You could even take that audio and open an iTunes account so that you drip feed your content as a weekly podcast. iTunes has a massive market of people looking for content to listen to on their iPods while they go about their lives. You never know, some of your future customers could be listening to you while they shop, ride the train or while they're working out in the gym. Be a superstar in your own right.

You could have a regular slot where you add new content weekly and gain your own group of followers.

http://www.apple.com/itunes/whatson/podcasts/fanfaq.html

Why stop there? Video is huge right now because media that engages the audio and visual senses is more attention grabbing than the written word alone. We are a generation that is accustomed with video and because it is such a natural part of our lives and a medium we all recognize, it makes sense to use it.

There are several ways to do this:

Video yourself talking about your product. These days most people have access to digital video cameras. You can easily upload your video to the multiple video sharing sites online.

You just import your video into Windows Movie Maker if you use Windows or iMovie if you use a Mac using a firewire IEEE 34 video card. This allows you to transfer big chunks of video to your computer in real time ready to edit. You can add titles to your footage. You can keep it simple, you don't need any Hollywood style special effects to make your video effective, just you, some titles, a little music and your imagination. Once you complete your video you can save it to MPEG, AVI, MP4, WMV, ASF, MOV to name a few of the recognized formats accepted by You-Tube then create an account and upload your video. They also have a new feature where you can mass upload videos to YouTube through their special new plug-in.

Always make sure that the videos you upload are original and are your own work.

http://www.youtube.com/my_videos_multiupload

You can submit videos up to 10 minutes in length on youtube.com and up to 1GB in size. If you want to create longer videos then I would suggest submitting to youtube.com and for mass submissions to other video sharing sites I would keep the length to a couple of minutes and the file size to under 100 MB. This is because the video sharing sites each have different file size maximums and when mass submitting keeping your video under a certain size will enable it to get accepted more readily.

You could even create little mini snippets of video about your product, upload to www.youtube.com and embed the video on your web page. Having video on your webpage can increase your opt in subscription rates and sales conversions. Getting subscribers to opt in to your ezine newsletter allows you to build a relationship with them and offer them quality products on a regular basis. This is where you want your business to be and building a long term solution that enables you to keep in regular content with your subscribers should be your long term goal.

http://www.youtube.com/sharing

In addition to creating video and placing it on your site, if you're a little shy you can create your video using Camstudio http://camstudio.org

Tutorial: http://www.youtube.com/watch?v=Kiug3H3c4gk

or Camtasia http://www.techsmith.com/camtasia.asp

Camstudio has some of the basic functions Camtasia does and best of all, it's free. Camstudio lets you film anything on your computer screen, this is a great feature for giving tutorials and giving demonstrations and talking about your products. This is also great for embedding in your web site and for mass submitting to video sharing sites.

If you want your videos to jump out at your viewers, here is some professional, completely royalty free music you can use that doesn't sound like those cheesy midi files of the late 80's and early 90's. If you want your slideshow video to sound like an old version of Donkey Kong or Super Mario Brothers then midi's got your name on it but if you want something a little more sophisticated then try: http://incompetech.com/m/c/royalty-free

The artist has very graciously made his music available to anyone wanting to use it, you just have read his terms of use and just give him credit in your work. His stuff is great and he composes all of his own tunes and loops on his site.

Here's another good link:
http://free-loops.com/download-free-loop-5599.html

If you have iMovie then you probably also have Garage band, this has lots of royalty free beats and loops you can use in your videos and they sound great too.

If the whole black and white look with music is a little bland and you absolutely don't want to narrate your own video then you can add pictures and get someone else to do the narration for you.

You can purchase stock photos from www.istockphoto.com for as little as $1 each. Because you are using these pictures for your own personal use and are not reselling them, you have permission to use them.

Here are the permitted uses for istockphoto's images:

(c) Permitted Uses. Subject to the restrictions described under Prohibited Uses below, the following are "Permitted Uses" of Content:

1. advertising and promotional projects, including printed materials, product packaging, presentations, film and video presentations, commercials, catalogues, brochures, promotional greeting cards and promotional postcards (i.e. not for resale or license);
2. entertainment applications, such as books and book covers, magazines, newspapers, editorials, newsletters, and video, broadcast and theatrical presentations;
3. on–line or electronic publications, including web pages to a maximum of 800 x 600 pixels;
4. prints, posters (i.e. a hardcopy) and other reproductions for personal use or promotional purposes specified in (1) above, but not for resale, license or other distribution; and
5. any other uses approved in writing by iStockphoto.

For the narration side you have a choice of several professional actors that can voiceover your video for you. Visit their site and you will be able to listen to voice over samples. Much of their talent are multi faceted and are able to read in different tones and styles. Go to www.voicetalentnow.com and check it out.

They charge $50 for a 30 to 60 second spot. Not bad considering it cost thousands to do this in a regular sound recording studio with voice talent.

I've used them on several occasions and they usually deliver within 48 to 72 hours. You give them a copy of your written script via email. Read it over and make sure that you time yourself. It can't stretch too far over your 60 second time slot. If it does your voice talent will just read it a little faster so that it fits within the 60 second allotted time frame. What you don't want to do is squeeze 2 minutes into 1 a minute recording, it will sound too rushed and your customers will lose precious information.

Once you read it over, trim the fat by getting rid of any information or unclear dialogue you don't need so that your 60 second script is as good as it possibly can be. Then all you do is fill out the order form where you specify which talent you liked best based upon their audio samples. You also include a couple of other choices in case they aren't available at that time. You pay your $50 through PayPal and you're away.

A few days later you will receive your voice recording. The great thing is that they give you 3 different voiceover styles for you to choose from.

All you do from that point on is upload it to your Windows Movie Maker or iMovie timeline and synch it with your pictures and your written titles. You can also add your music too but keep it low in the background so that your visitors can every word of dialogue and it doesn't distract them from taking the action of signing up as a subscriber or checking out your product. Then add it to your web page.

What you can then do with all of these videos is burn them to DVD and use them as promotional tools for your products very effective especially with your little 60 second professionally voiced promotional teaser.

Don't forget you don't have to go to the lengths of having a professional voice over artist, research shows that people tend to react just as strongly to videos and audios where a real person is narrating. They are able to readily more connect with that person. The voiceover route is there for you if it's something you feel more comfortable doing.

Did you know that if you decide to transform your product into an audio CD or DVD that you don't need to hassle with posting them out to your clients? Pretty fantastic eh? Who wants to mess around with filling orders and running to the post office everyday when you don't have to?

www.kunaki.com takes care of that for you. You just send them your audio or video file uploaded as an MP3 file or MPEG4, mov, wav, etc when you fill out the form on their web site. Kunaki can produce an outstanding, high quality physical product in jewel casing from your digital file for around $1.75 each and for as low as $5.00 each including drop shipping directly to your customer. They fulfill all orders on your behalf which means no trips to the post office and the price is reasonable. You pay Kunaki the amount for the product plus drop shipping and you keep the rest.

This is great if you've chosen a private label rights product to fully revamp but what if you chose a master resell rights product instead? How do we make it new without altering it?

As we touched upon before you could write your own related ebook to accompany your resell rights product. You could create a mini report as a review to accompany your master resell rights product. Very powerful when you give a personal endorsement and it carries more weight from you as a user.

You should also try the products; give your own perspective on them. If it's software write what it was like to use, how easy was it to navigate? did you save you time?, did it serve a purpose or fulfill a need? If was an ebook how did it help you? what tips did you apply and what was your outcome?

This is also a great way to know if the product does what it claims to do and you have tried and tested proof to back it with.

Did that Article Content Creator really save you time? Was it user friendly? was it all it claimed to be? What were your likes and dislikes? Do you give a balanced viewpoint not every product can be 100% perfect and you won't come across as all sales pitchy like you would if you have nothing but praise for the product, people become skeptical and think that you're just trying to make the sale rather than what's in their best interest. That's not to say that there are genuine products out there that really do live up to their expectations. Just be honest and fair.

If the product doesn't live up to its claims it's best you don't promote it anyway. Remember, you're establishing a reputation which will be like currency later on and people will buy based upon the strength of your recommendation alone.

So start writing your own review, it's a quick way to get started and you don't need testimonials because you are the testimonial. If you give details of the product you tested and provide social proof of your success people will buy from you.

After completing your mini report you should then convert it to PDF (Portable Document Format) which is the most widely used format for sending and reading information on the internet, .exe ebooks have the disadvantage of being unreadable on Mac operating systems. It's best to stick with PDF so that you can access a global audience without any limitations.

Free versions are great to start with if you're producing a mini report but they have their limitations, they lack a lot of the functions that the paid versions have and can only produce reports of up to a maximum size of 1-3 MB, not suitable if you want to create larger ebooks with graphics.

www.openoffice.org works extremely well and has had lots of positive reviews and is free.

I'm very happy using www.cutepdf.com. It's not free but for only $49.95 is very affordable and with a sale or two you've easily made back your money.

Another reason why I like Cute PDF is that it preserves links when viewing from a Mac operating system through Preview, the equivalent of windows Adobe reader, whereas some PDF converters don't.

If you decide to go with Cute PDF you simply install the software upon pur-chase. When it comes time to convert your word document to PDF format the icon appears as a print engine. You select it and within 10 seconds you have a readymade PDF ready to go.

Don't forget to run your ebook through your spell checker. Forgive me if I missed a few spelling errors myself along the way, I tend to write quickly so a few may have slipped through the net.

Getting Feedback on Your New, Improved Resell Rights Product

Your product is a work in progress and there are always bound to be changes along the way. Don't be disheartened, it's the changes and alterations that make it an increasingly better product which can only serve you in the long run, right?

If you have been participating on the warrior forum and digitalpoint forum why not ask some people to review it for you and give you unbiased feedback.

There are plenty of people that would be willing to do that for you. Give out say 10 copies and wait for their feedback. You may want to take any considerations and make any necessary changes. Also if feedback is really good ask if you could use it as a testimonial on your site.

If you are not given permission to publish their comments or if you are unable to get anyone to review your product then just go on the strength of your product alone and let your customers be the judge. If they like your product and email you commenting on it then politely ask if you can use it as a testimonial on your site. These are the strongest kinds of testimonials because they are from legitimate customers.

Naked Sales Copy - Copywriting Exposed

Sounds a little provocative don't it? But it's true. We're going to strip it bare and get right down to the anatomy of great sales copy. Sounds like an episode of CSI but trust me you're going to enjoy the ride.

Now, we're going to get a head start on our copywriting because most of the hard work's already been done for us.

Take a look at the resell product you've chosen to re-create paying particular attention to the graphics, the sales page (if any) and the written ad copy within the sales page. If you're not sure where to find the sales page it's usually called "index.hml" or "sales.html".

Grab some ideas from the headline and the sales copy. Take note of the main points that grab your attention and paste it into a word document file.

Most of the leg work is already done for you. The creators of these products have already singled out all of the strong points of their products. Do they have an eye catching, magnetizing headline that reels you in? Chances are if it works on you it will work on your target market.

Do they weave a story that draws you in or does it offer hard hitting in your face fact? Do they highlight benefits? do they remove all of your objections by addressing any questions and doubts you may have? Do they offer you piece of mind with a money back guarantee? Will it shape your life? What does it promise to do? Does it bring happiness or remove pain? Will it give you a better quality of life? will it simplify your life? Does it offer solutions to your existing problems?

Sounds intense doesn't it? But it's true everyone is looking for a silver bullet to their problems and if your product can help them you've got a winner.

"Sorry But 3 Seconds Is All You Got, Period"

Imagine attending the most crucial job interview of your entire life and all the time you had to wow your future employer was 3 seconds, what would you say? You'd make every word count, that's for sure.

Your sales copy is no different.

Instead of your employer you have your prospective customer and you still have those same 3 seconds to win them over.

What would you say? What if your life depended upon it? Let me tell you that it would be a lot different than your usual old sales pitch.

You would choose your words very carefully especially if they were your last.

Why do I ask? because this is how we should write our ad copy. Treat those words if they were the last you were ever to utter. Treat them as though they were the last you were going to speak to the love about to leave your life forever and you only had 3 seconds to make them stay.

You only ever get one shot, once it's gone, it's gone. So you have to make it count. No pressure.

So why is it so important to grab your prospects by the eyeballs immediately? because we only have only 3 seconds before they click away to the next page.

3 seconds! No lie. There is a constant war being waged for our attention on a daily basis. The weapons of choice being television, billboard, radio, newspaper and most recently the internet.

Online, we have to compete with the next site which is always just a click away. We have only 3 precious seconds to hook our visitor's attention so it's extremely important that we make those words count because it's these words that will convert into product sales.

The Anatomy of Good Sales Copy

To write good copy you've got to learn what good copy is.

I can't stress the importance of writing your own sales copy even if it is when you're first starting out.

The reason is because you need to recognize the elements of successful copy so that you can apply it to your own.

Even if you outsource to a professional, only you really know your product inside and out better than anyone else. The copywriter will still need your input anyways so best do it yourself so you can get a feel for writing your own good copy.

If you do decide to eventually outsource at least you have an idea of what makes successful copy and why it works. This also gives you a solid foundation to makes changes to your own ad copy if it's been outsourced because even professionals don't always get it 100% right.

Your sales copy must be done right. It doesn't matter if you have the best thing since sliced bread. If you can't hook them with your sales copy, they'll never find out.Don't worry if you've never written sales copy before, it's a great skill to develop and I promise you, great copyrighters are more often made then born.

You don't have to worry if your sales copy isn't perfect either. It doesn't have to be. This is thing that stops people from even putting their own products out there because it's the notion that everything has to be 100% perfect straight out of the gate, rubbish. How are you supposed to know what's perfect until you take it for a test drive and smooth off the rough edges as you go?

It's in the doing that the perfection comes. You will begin to see what works and what doesn't for yourself. You will be able to test, tweak and refine until you can't improve your ad copy any further. You can only do that when your product is out there in the trenches collecting real data and not still stuck in the hangar being spit polished until you can see your reflection in it. So don't be afraid to take chances and get your product and sales copy out there, you'll be miles ahead if you do.

Tone

Huh? People don't think about tone when it comes to copywriting yet tone is just as important as the words that express it.

Tone is more a subconscious element but it's important when you have a message to get across. Tone sets the mood of your sales copy. Are you trying to convey positive, fun and upbeat? or are you going more for solemn, sobering and factual? Or are you perhaps trying to educate, clarify and teach?

Your tone is what permeates through your ad copy. Your excitement, passion, enthusiasm is what hooks people, it's the subconscious meaning on a deeper level that is more far reaching than words alone.

Ever hear the expression that excitement is contagious? It's a fact. The energy that comes from your ad copy will excite and charge your customers that they'll want to experience it for themselves and take action.

Don't bore your visitors, energize them. Why do you think the likes of Anthony Robbins, the late Steve Irwin and yes, even Gordon Ramsey have huge followings? because you can sense their passion for what they do.

How do we create the right tone?

Get excited about your product.

If you have followed all of the steps up to this point with your product research and development you will create a product worthy of praise. You will be able to feel confident about what you are promoting.

This is why we researched it so thoroughly and left no stone unturned in making it better than it was before. This should give you all the confidence you need, knowing that you back a fantastic quality product that people will want.

So be excited with your tone, excited that this is something you're about to share that will help improve their life in some way, to add value whether it's to save time, save money, to educate, to improve, to lose weight or to win over the love of their life this is the product for them.

Write in a conversational tone just as I am with you, just like how you would talk over a cup of coffee, this will ensure you connect with your reader on a personal level like you would a friend.

Research shows that you need to give people a reason why to listen to you and that couldn't be truer seeing as you're just a bunch of words on a screen.

Don't forget to always address why your prospects should read your sales copy. People are suspicious creatures by nature and need a reason to trust you. They need to know why they should listen to and trust you. What knowledge do you have that can help them? How can you make their life easier? What's in it for them?

Always try to answer that question in your copy by removing their objections and you'll have gained their trust.

The Most Important Factor in Your Sales Copy – Failure to Get This Right Will Kill Your Sales

If I were to sum up the most important part of the sales copy it would be the headline, hands down. Why do we give such weight to headlines? Because it's the first thing your prospects see.

If your headline fails to grab no matter how incredible your product nobody will ever know because your visitor won't even have made it past the first paragraph let alone all the way down the page to your order button. Not hooking your prospects from the start with your headline will kill your sales.

The Headline 80/20 Rule

Just like the 80/20 rule that states that 20% of people will do 80% of the selling when it comes to affiliate marketing, headlines have an 80/20 rule of their own that states that 80% of your visitors will read your headline and only 20% will make it to the end of your sales copy.

If your headline is terrible then that number will be dramatically less which will impact your sales so make sure that your headline grabs from the start, using buzz words that make people react will give you the upper hand.

Getting down to the bare bones of copywriting, all great sales copy really is is just a series of successfully completed stages designed to convert into a sale and that's it. It begins with your sucker punch headline which leads visitors to your sub headline, introduction, body copy, features and benefits, guarantee, order button, sale.

Each element is designed to move your visitor onto the next stage like a conveyor belt, some will jump off and some will continue on until the remaining 2% left on your sales page finally click through to the order page and buy your product.

Your headline is what makes visitors stay on your sales page for longer than those first crucial 3 seconds get past this and you greatly increase your chances of making that sale. Don't nail it and no matter how fantastic your product is they'll never make it far down enough on your sales page to even order it.

That's why it's vital to start with a take no prisoners headline. Done right can increase your sale by up 1,500% or more.
So what exactly makes a great headline?

Anything that invokes a thought, a gut reaction, a response and drives your reader to take a desired course of action.

The best headlines arouse emotions, curiosity, excite and titillate.

8 Types of Headline

Your headline is bound to fit into one or more of these headline types.

1. The Benefit Driven Headline

As you can guess this is a headline that addresses a benefit and is only as effective as the knowledge you have of your market.

Knowing your target market allows you to uncover what makes them tick and what will keep them glued to your ad.

Find as many benefits as you can and only use the strongest, most compelling one from your list.

We'll discuss benefits in greater detail as we go, but for now they are what drive your prospect to act on your offer by adding a layer of emotional appeal.

For example:

"Are you a prisoner chained to your business? Free yourself and let us do the hard slog for you. 100% fully automated software takes care of all of the work so you can live your life."

The benefit here being more time, no longer being tied to your business. More time with family and to do the things you love most in life. Who doesn't want more time to themselves? No one likes to think they're tied unwillingly to anything so whatever addresses this issue will work well.

2. The Testimonial Headline

This is one of the most powerful headlines because it contains proof in the form of a real customer testimonial.

For example:
"I had heard of the promises and claims that your product worked and because of your money back guarantee I decided to give it a try. I'm glad I did because within 7 days I lost 3 pounds and 2 inches off my waist. All I can say is I would highly recommend your product to anyone wanting to try it".
Mary Alice

Las Vegas

(Email address)

Headlines with celebrity testimonials work well but not as well as from regular people. This is because people know that celebrities sometimes get paid to endorse products and having a celebrity back a product stretches reality for some unless they back a reputable product with a solid track record that's been on the market for some time. There would be no doubt if say Bruce Willis backed the Bow flex simply by its reputation alone.

A well known expert in your products field works well, for example a top fisherman endorsing your bass fishing techniques product definitely draws attention.

3. The Discount Sale Headline

This is the most obvious headline. What you see is what you get. No clever double meanings or hard hitting words. Great for announcing fire sales and discount specials.

For example:

"50% Discount On Everything In Store, But Hurry Sale Ends Midnight"

Here's how to add some spin on this particular style of headline by adding the power of "why" which makes sense to your prospect.

For example:

"Our shipment of women's summer shoes arrived 3 weeks too late and now we've got to get rid of them to make way for the winter collection. Help us clear out some storage space and we'll thank you by giving you free pair of shoes with every pair you purchase."

Getting specific, weaving a little story and giving a strong reason why they should order that makes sense will get your prospects to jump at your offer. Your prospect gets what they want while feeling good that they're helping you out at the same time, win-win.

4. The News Driven Headline

This headline packs a lot of clout because it mimics the exclusive press release format plugging a new product. This is a good way to go if the product is brand new on the market.

"Groundbreaking New System Delivers Hands Down
The Quickest Way To Tone Your Abdominals, Shrink
Your Thighs And Buttocks And Burn Pounds Of Fat --
All While You Watch Television"

When using news headlines push benefits, notice how we didn't go into the specifics of the product itself but rather the results the product produced, that's what people want to know, what it can do for them.

5. The "How To" Headline

A "how to" headline might be the thing if your product reveals how to do something. Most products fall into this category, whether you want to learn how to catch more fish, make more money, lose weight, be more attractive to the opposite sex, gain more confidence, improve health, look younger this is the headline for you.

For example:
"How To Attract And Win Over Any Woman Without Fail
Even If You're A Complete Loser –
And She Was Way Out Of Your League"

6. The Guarantee Headline

Rather than wait for your prospects to find your guarantee further down on your sales page you're hitting them with it right up front.

"Attention Fishing Enthusiasts -- We Guarantee You Will Catch
At Least 50% More Fish With The Cutting Edge Techniques You're
About To Discover Or You Get Your Money Back!"

Your product must be that good if you come out punching with your guarantee.

Quotation marks give authenticity to your statement because it's represents a real, live person speaking directly to you, so use them for most of your headlines if you can.

7. The Solution Headline

Once you know your market you can identify the biggest problem plaguing them and offer a solution. Making them aware of that problem plucks them right out of the general population and speaks personally to them.

"If Your Computer Hard Drive Were To Suddenly Crash While
You Were Reading This, Would It Bring Your Business To Its Knees?
How To Make Sure This Never Happens To You"

Common problems and fears people face that you might want to address in your headline:
- **job security**
- **health issues**
- **lack of money**
- **appearance**
- **personal life**
- **love life**
- **friends**
- **status**

8. The Question Asking Headline

This type of headline relies heavily upon your research.

Just like giving your benefit upfront because you know your prospects objections, the question headline works in a similar way.

This time you're getting into their heads and asking the same questions on their minds and offering solutions to them. If done well, they'll think you read their mind. Remember to be clear and specific and you'll be able to connect with your prospect like you were speaking to them directly. It makes them feel important.

"Are You Fed Up To The Eyeballs With All Of the Pills,
Potions and Plans That Still Keep You Over Fat and Under Fit?"

"With All Of The Dieting Has It Really Made You Any Slimmer?"

"Have You Noticed That Your Diet Has Made You Fatter?"

Powerful questions that address the issue with dieting compelling your prospect to want to know more because you just spoke to them directly by describing their frustration.

So there you have it, any headline you will ever create will fall into one or more of these categories. Don't be afraid to experiment and use any of these elements to create your own.

So what makes a phenomenal headline? , we need to know what a phenomenal headline looks like.

The 5 Greatest Headlines of All Time

Believe it or not but these are the top 5 direct marketing headlines in history. They've been responsible for selling mega millions of dollars worth of products throughout the years.

The common theme that connects of all these headlines is that they raise curiosity and they've all been written in very plain, simple English.

The reason to keep your language plain is because the reading level that the average American is accustomed to reading is at around the 8th grade mark.

This isn't to say that they can't read at a 10th or 12th grade level or higher but simply because they don't have the time to. Most people are so busy that they don't have the time to sift through flowery, expressive language. Check out commercials and listen to the language being used to see what I mean.

Your writing should stir emotion and cause your prospect to take action not to draw attention to itself. Complicated, drawn out, longwinded language distracts and will cause your prospects to lose interest.

So aim to your language at the 8th grade level when writing your sales copy.

1."They laughed when I sat down at the piano - but when I started to play!"

The number one, best selling headline of all time responsible for grossing hundreds of millions of dollars in sales over the past 50 plus years.

Why it works:

Everyone loves a great story, from the time we are children we've been conditioned to love them. We want to know what happens next, that coupled with the curiosity factor hooks people in and keeps them reading. It's our nature as human beings to be curious; we want to know what people's reactions were when he started to play the piano so we get hooked in for the ride.

This headline still works and only requires a modern day adjustment to suit your own product. Writing great copy can be as simple as borrowing from the best. Knowing what works and then making a few alterations to fit your own sales copy. You just got a thousand dollar copywriting education from standing on the shoulders of giants, free.

For example:
"They laughed when I told them I make money online - but when
I showed them my PayPal account!"

How's that for curiosity and with the proof to boot? People will be reading just to know how much this person made and was it really so much it stopped the laughing dead in its tracks?

Put your own spin on it.

Practice by slotting in your own words, you have a multimillion dollar headline for free here, so put it to good use.

"They laughed when I _____ but when I _____!"

2. They grinned when the waiter spoke to me in French - but their laughter changed to amazement at my reply.

This is very similar to the first headline and works for the same reasons.

This time it's French instead of piano, reply instead of playing resulting in both groups having the laughter shocked out of them with amazement.

It's basically just a modified version of the first headline, proving it works just as well even when changing the situation.

Again it's the curiosity factor that draws the reader in. They want to know why the people were amazed. What did the person say to the waiter that caused the laughter to turn to astonishment?

3. Do you make these mistakes in English?

I still see this headline everywhere today in many different forms because it has so many applications, i.e. do you make these mistakes with the opposite sex? do you make these mistakes in your business?, do you make these mistakes with your diet?

People will do anything in life to do either of two things, to achieve pleasure or to avoid pain. Being aware of your mistakes helps you to avoid the pain of embarrassment, loneliness, humiliation, financial loss, heartache, failure, unhappiness.

This is why this very simple headline still works extremely well today because it appeals to the very basic human need to be accepted and we achieve this by avoiding the pain that comes from making mistakes.

Substitute your own words:
Do you make these mistakes in _____?

4. How a "fool stunt" made me a star salesman

People respond well to "How" type headlines and this one works particularly well because it sounds more like a story than just a headline. We want to know how a fool stunt could make anyone famous so we stick around and read the whole sales copy to find the answer.

You could use it this way:
How one "accidental mistake" made me a superstar copywriter.
How a "_____" made me a star _____

5. Free to brides - $2 to others

This appeals to pride, being a part of an exclusive group makes people feel special and superior, it's a headline that speaks directly to its targeted prospects, in this case to "brides". This is an effective method for targeting only the group that you want by singling them out.

Free to bus drivers - $__ to others
Free to dog owners - $__ to others
Free to scuba divers - $__ to others
Use your own:
Free to _____ $__ to others

Here are some of the top 100 headlines from Mr. Jay Abrahams, copywriting genius extraordinaire. Study them and get a feel for them. The more you use great headlines the more they will come naturally when writing your own.

http://www.abraham.com/articles/100_Greatest_Headlines_Ever_Written.html

Now that we've looked at 5 of the best headlines in history we're going to get down to the specifics of writing our own great headline.

Constructing a Brilliant Headline That Gets Read

Clayton Makepeace, copywriting master and guru taught that every great headline should satisfy 6 important questions in order to be a hit.

1. Does your headline offer the reader a reward for reading?
2. What specifics could you add to make your headline more intriguing and believable?
3. Does your headline trigger a strong, actionable emotion the reader already has about the subject at hand?
4. Does your headline present a proposition that will instantly get your prospect nodding his or her head?
5. Could your headline benefit from the inclusion of a proposed transaction?
6. Could you add an element of intrigue to drive the prospect into your opening copy?

Factoring in these questions when creating your headline will give you a strong foundation to build from and will ultimately help your headline pull better.

How to Make Your Headlines Jump off the Screen

As we discussed earlier we only have 3 seconds to get the job done and have our readers hooked which means the first 3 words of your head line are the most crucial so why not use the types of words that will grab them by the eyeballs?

Something with a little shock value. I used in the sales copy accompanying this report "Sick To Death", pretty strong words but well justified especially to a market fed up with not making a cent with resell rights products.

It is attention grabbing without being offensive or vulgar although there are some copywriters who like to offend the hell out of their readers and take great pride in it. It's funny because the more a reader gets angry and worked up the more of the sales copy they read.

They've been poked and prodded emotionally into taking action, whether it's buying the product, signing up to their newsletter or to write a letter of complaint, the writer just made you jump through a hoop and without you even knowing it.

It works for some copywriters because they know what they're doing but these are tactics much like the Rich Jerk that I prefer not to use, it's just not my style.

Be careful how you want to approach it, the same approach that can set you apart from the others can also get you tossed like dirty laundry. Use offensive tactical maneuvers with extreme caution, if done incorrectly can blow up in your face.

Another way to get inspiration for your copywriting is to just look at your email inbox. There's a truckload of them in there. The good, the bad and the ugly.

Keep note of the headlines that grab your attention to steal some of the best bits for your own.

Lots of the elements we discussed before are alive and well today in fact this is an email subject line I found in my inbox today from a marketer:

"Average Joe Makes $644.77 a day".

How's that for specific? And average Joe means that anyone can do it.

Copywriting Basics 101

Give attention to action or impact words in your headline by emphasizing them with a different color and by capitalizing each new word.

BIG, Bold Lettering

(Times New Roman, Verdana, Arial and Georgia are fonts that work well, 36 size font, deeper red RGB (192, 0, 0).

Don't be shy to use red because not only does it grab your readers attention but we have been conditioned to recognize that we are about to be sold something so it gets your readers into a state of mind.

Buzz Words That Hook Your Reader and Reels Them In

Here is a whole list of buzz words that are proven to snatch your reader's attention. Feel free to use them to pimp your headlines.

Amazing	Burning	Frenzy
Astonish	Quick	Steal
Breakthrough	Instant	Incredible
Revolutionary	Direct	Proven
Shocking	Overnight	Secret
Brand New	Scorching	Covert
How To	Tips	Explicit
Miracle	Technique	Painless
Limited Time Only	Sizzling	Effortless
Discovery	Opportunity	Straightforward
Revealed	Guaranteed	Easy
Exposed	Greatest	Simple
Naked	Supreme	Fastest
Concealed	Maximum	Best

Free	Confident	Thrilling
Hot	Renewed	Captivating
Certain	Complimentary	Released
Definite	Limitless	Immediate
Surefire	Liberated	Revelation
Exact	Freedom	Mind Blowing

If you get stuck for inspiration and need more words, just grab a word from the list and plug it into your thesaurus for more alternatives.

- 5 _____ to win over friends and influence people _____
  5 techniques to win over friends and influence people released
  5 tips to win over friends and influence people guaranteed

- _____ ad copy _____

Naked ad copy exposed
Hot ad copy revealed
Captivating ad copy released
Practice writing your headlines, you have everything within your grasp to create cash pulling headlines that the process will become automatic, you'll even be dreaming of great headlines so keep a notepad and pen beside your bed.

Since writing ad copy I notice headlines everywhere now. I analyze them to see why they work or how they could be made better and it will become second nature to you too.

Headline Length – How Long Is Too Long?

Headline length is not an issue, 8 words or 20 words, if well targeted and attention grabbing, both work equally as well. It depends on what you're trying to convey.

I came across a sales letter with a 30 word headline today and yes it looked a little long but for what it communicated worked well with the word length.

Back in the old days headlines were usually no longer than 8 words in length because of the limited space in print magazines. These days with the webpage you have a lot more room to play with. Generally if you can fit your headline into a sentence then do so but if you need to write more, 2 sentences should do the trick. Some copywriters use an entire paragraph for their headline, if it's loaded with a benefit and achieves its purpose of encouraging the reader to continue reading then that's fine too.

Stories Sell Products

Now that we devoted a good chunk of time to get our headline right now we get down to the nitty-gritty of your sales copy.

Immediately following your headline should be a short little sub-headline, this is a teaser for your headline enticing your visitors to read more.

Then you get right into your sales copy with either compelling questions to make your prospect think or get straight into your introduction which serves the purpose of explaining your headline in more depth without giving too much away.

Your sales copy should be a story because stories sell.

We all love to hear a great story especially if it answers a burning question asked in the headline. Stories also paint a picture with mental imagery and allow the reader to get involved.

Note: To establish credibility, add a photo of yourself on your site, your email address and phone number. People like to know they're dealing with real people and if they have any problems they find comfort in knowing they can contact you. This is great for building trust.

Before you write your ad copy you first need to think of your market.

The sales copy your write for nursing mothers would be a lot different than for truck drivers. By this point you would have already determined your market because as I teach you would never be at the point of writing sales copy without first knowing this. This is crucial to your sales success.

After your headline your introduction you need to keep your readers keen by building on, revealing little details and juicy tidbits as your story progresses on without giving away the farm.

Target your audience and speak to them. Tell them how your life was before you created your product. Tell them why you created it in the first place and what kind of frustrating circumstances your product was born from; chances are they feel the same frustrations too.

Tell them how your life has changed as result and how their life can change too.

You can relate to them because you were in their shoes but being on the other side is so much better and you now get to enjoy more freedom, more money, eat whatever you want and still lose weight, more attractive to the opposite sex, more popular, more friends, save money and time.

As long as you can weave an interesting little back story into your copy you will maintain a captive audience going along for the ride with you.

Always be truthful, never try to sell anything that doesn't live up to your expectations, it has to do what you claim it does or your refund rate will be high and you don't want that.
Always be honest, all you're doing is selling a great product you know there is a market for.

Don't forget to:

• Know your market
• Know their frustrations, objections, barriers and challenges
• Consult yahoo answers to get specific questions then place them in your headline and proceed to answer them in your ad copy without giving everything away.

Your visitors question "What are the best bass fishing techniques at depths of 15 feet?"

Headline "Best Bass Fishing Techniques of All Time Even At Depths of 15 Feet Or Less".

You've addressed their question and are promising to provide an answer. Why wouldn't they read on especially since you apparently read their mind?

A Thousand Dollar Tip For Free

There have been times when I've been pulled in so strongly by the sales copy of a product that I buy it, then thud, huge disappointment because none of the passion was captured in the ebook itself. It almost seemed like the sales copy was from mars and the product from Venus, they just didn't fit. I just expect my product to be as great as the sales copy.

Tip – if your sales copy talks up your product just make sure your product delivers it.

This is an easy trap to fall into, you make a great product, you sell it up big time in your ad copy but then your ebook doesn't quite capture that same enthusiasm.

I write my sales copy. I do a few drafts until I feel it's where it should be. Then I go back to my ebook and assess if it's an accurate account of my product. I know my product is great it just needs to flow on smoothly from my sales copy.

The first page or two of your ebook should be a comfortable transition from your sales copy, think of it an extension of the sales copy itself.

Why?

Because your customers are so pumped and jazzed from your copy, enough that they took action and purchased right there and then. No doubt they'll be downloading your product straight off the bat and will want to tuck straight into your content.

What they want to feel is that high even after the sale, the excitement that got them to buy from you in the first place. They've just bought and they're still excited. So after writing your sales copy go back and rewrite the first few pages of your ebook so that it's a natural flow on from your copy and captures that energy.

I usually do a couple of drafts, then I leave it for a day or two to marinade and see if it still jumps out at me later on, so I can look at it with a fresh pair of eyes. If it doesn't pull me in, I rework it.

It's All in the Detail

After knowing your market and their most burning questions and objections which you can then go on to address throughout your story, you may want to use specifics.

Specific detail = real world, because nothing in life is perfect and tidy.

Specific = believable.

Which sounds more realistic?

(a). "Using the secret bass fishing technique I thought my fishing line was possessed, I caught 10 fish each with an average weight of 10 pounds."

(b). "Using the secret bass fishing technique I thought my fishing line was possessed, I caught 10 fish with the smallest being 9 pounds, 3 ounces all the way up to 10 pounds and 7 ounces."

They both come to the same figure but they were expressed differently. The second one stands out as being real because weights are very rarely perfect in the real world.

Don't be afraid to describe and list details.
Which sounds more believable?

(A). "In the last 7 days I pulled in $10,000 in sales".

(b). "In the last 7 days I pulled in $10,036.22 in sales".

Don't forget details because it's what gives your sales copy credibility.

The Long and the Short of It

How long should your copy be? in answer, as long as it needs to be.

Before making a major purchase people want as much information as possible to make an informed buying decision.

Generally the more expensive a product the longer the sales copy required to convince. They have no prior knowledge of you; they don't know you from a bar of soap so you need longer to earn their trust. The positive is that the longer they stay on your webpage and read through your long sales copy, the more likely they will be to buy.

Another reason for long sales copy is to plug products that are brand new on the market. Especially products no one has prior knowledge of.

The long copy is to educate your prospect on why the product is needed. Just like cell phones. What was the point of having a cell phone to keep in touch with your family when nobody even had them yet?

There was no one to phone; you would have had a more effective system of communication if you used 2 cups and a piece of string.

But there you have it. People were educated on how they could be useful that everyone bought them just to say they had one. Nowadays people can't live without their cell phones. How's that for 180 degree turnaround?

For products over $297 I would go for a (10 plus page sales letter)

Products $97 - $296 (5 pages – 10 pages)

Products under $96 (around 5 pages)
These aren't rock solid, set in stone rules, and just like Captain Barbossa from the Pirates of the Caribbean - Curse of the Black Pearl says "They're not rules they're more guidelines".

Treat it as such. The only way to know for sure is to do some testing. Use different sales copy length to see what converts best for you and your offers.

Featuring the Benefits

When will people learn that we sell to live, breathing human beings and that it's emotions that seal the deal?

People aren't buying a product they're buying a feeling, they're buying an emotion, a peace of mind. The psychology of why people buy is more far reaching than you can ever comprehend.

I remember reading an article about a marketer whose product was to teach people how to make money.

The incredible thing was that most never applied his system, had they done so they would have enjoyed making money for real. Funny thing was when interviewed as to why they never applied the system their response was that just having it sitting on their book shelves where they could see it gave them hope and comfort that at any given moment they could apply the system and make money.

They just wanted to own the system; the feeling knowing they owned it was enough to satisfy them, incredible isn't it? the human psyche.

We won't delve too deep into the psychology behind it, that's psyche 101 territory but believe me, the take home message is, people don't buy products, they buy feelings.

Look at the car, people don't purchase a hunk of metal for the sake of it but how it will make them feel, to get attention and admiration to win respect and to elevate their status and social standing.

Weight loss products, people purchase them to lose weight why? to feel better about themselves, to increase their self confidence levels and ultimately to be loved and accepted.

Recipes, sure they are delicious but do you think that's the only reason why people buy them? How about being able to show off to their friends the level of skill they possess in the kitchen? How about being able to impress family and friends with the new culinary dishes when all they could do a week ago was boil water badly? How about being the only one out of all their friends to have a recipe for "The Best Chocolate Cake in the World"? Imagine whipping out that ace come birthday time, they would be the envy of all their friends.

People want to make money from home, why? You will find it's not just for the fancy cars and houses or for the sake of making more money but for how it makes them feel. More independence, more time with family, relaxed, stress free, peace of mind especially during the current economic climate.

Perfume is a classic example, would women flock to buy perfume named "Some

Brownish Liquid That Makes You Smell Good"?, of course not even though that's all perfume really is but package it nicely and call it "Goddess" and who wouldn't want a piece of that?

Kimora Lee Simmons doesn't sell perfume, she sells attitude and she generates hundreds of millions of dollars in revenue each year because of it. Her perfume flies off shelves not because women want yet another bottle to clog up their bathroom sinks but because they want a taste of being a "Goddess". They buy it because of how it will make them feel. Attitude in a 3.4 ounce bottle.

You are selling feelings and emotions, there is nothing more powerful and the best copywriters in history knew this.

What helps to sell product are benefits. By the time you finish with this you'll be able to pick out all of the benefits from any existing ad copy and get inspiration from them for your own.

The Purpose of Benefits and Features

Feature – A feature outlines facts, specifications, statistics or characteristics about a product. They are neutral in that they don't sell products alone because don't address the question we all have and that's "what's in it for me?"

For example – "Shopping cart has the new 1 click order feature."

(Well that's great, but what does that mean for me? why should I care? how can that benefit me?)

When features work on their own:

This is more cut out for people who understand specifications and facts and are satisfied with being supplied with them alone usually because it's within their profession or their field of expertise or field of knowledge.

For example for Photographer's the Canon SX10 IS has a powerful extended zoom and it features a long, 20x optical zoom and a 28-56 wide angle lens with image stabilization a 2.5 inch swivel LCD screen and 10 megapixel resolution. Video speed 30fps, Focus Range 19.2 in. to Infinity (w) / 39.6 in. to Infinity (t), Focal Length 5 - 100 mm, File size 4.22 MB, etc.

Means nothing to the average person but to a photographer a dream come true.

Benefit – A benefit is what sells. It gives your features meaning, something that your customer can connect with and transforms features into solutions.

Benefits push emotional hot buttons which satisfy the "what's in it for me" question. Benefits get your customers to imagine how their life would be improved using your product so you're really selling emotions which is far more powerful than cold hard fact.

Benefits in the case of our camera are maximum scope and coverage with extended zoom no matter how far in the distance your object is. You can store plenty of pictures with the 4.22 MB file size meaning that you can take even more pictures. Video speed of 30 fps closely resembles real film quality meaning that your video will have a professional look to it. 10 megapixel resolution means clearer crisper quality images, etc.

Benefit for our 1 click order feature – "The 1 click order feature allows your customer to order safely, quickly and easily from you without hassle. It makes for an easy, pleasant ordering process which will keep your customers ordering from you again and again. They'll never have to fill in another order form when they order from you ever again."

See the difference? Features outline facts but Benefits sell emotions and feelings. Benefits put your customer in the driving seat to experience how their life would be improved owning your product. If your benefit makes them feel good, they'll buy from you.

Example: The Article Content Creator

Feature: Create articles in 1/10th of the time.

Benefit: "Having the article content creator is like buying more hours in the day. It slashes the amount of work you do by 10 times. Who doesn't want more time with family? the driving range?, or to just grow your business more? It's like having an army of people doing the work for you."

Compelling because you give people a reason to buy and you show them what's in it for them and how it can improve the quality of their lives.

If I have several benefits listed I usually bullet them and alternate between bold and plain for each separate benefit, this enables each benefit to stand out in its own right.
Use as many benefits as you have, the more the merrier. But make sure they make an impact and move your prospects to the sale.

Have strongest benefits at the top and bottom and the weakest ones in the middle. In psychology there is a process called the "Primacy and Recency Effect".

What that means is that when given a page full of details people remember what they read at the beginning and at the end but forgot the middle. That's why it's important to have your strongest points at the beginning and at the end because it's what your prospect will be most likely to remember.

For example:

☑ **Benefit One**
☑ **Benefit Two**
☑ **Benefit Three**
☑ **Benefit Four**
☑ **Benefit Five**

Testimonials

If you have them, use them. They provide social proof that your product works which removes even more of your prospects objections.

The testimonials that work the least effectively are ones that don't have full names, you know the ones I'm talking about, the ones that look like this:

"I love your product, it helped me make 10 times more money"
S. Smith, Odessa, Texas.

I'm sorry but if there was anything to cast massive doubt on the authenticity of your product and even upon you as the products creator, it would be this kind of endorsement.

I never trust these because they turn me off from buying a product and it wouldn't be surprising if it failed to impress your prospect too.

Even if it is the only kind of testimonial you have, try for a more detailed one so that people know real people tried it.

Remember how earlier on you got people to review your product? Ask them if you can use their review on your website and if they could include their photo, website if any and email address.

The longer your product has been out there the more likely you are to get feedback from your customers. Any time you get a positive comment ask for permission if you can use it on your site.

The strongest type of testimonials includes proof your product works with pictures of the people endorsing your products so that your prospects know they're real. Audio testimonials work extremely well too with the strongest testimonials of all being video.

People love proof, the more compelling a testimonial, the more sales you'll make.

300% More Sales By Removing Objections

Something as simple as a money back guarantee can increase your sales by a whopping 300%.

A guarantee means that you stand by your product and that you're willing to put your money where your mouth is. It removes fear and objections your prospects may have towards trying your product and seals the deal.

Your sales copy should answer all of their questions, the only reason why they wouldn't buy even after sticking with your sales letter right to the bitter end is because you simply didn't answer all of their questions or they were left with doubt.

30 days is a reasonable time frame, 60 days works well too. Some people give 365 day guarantees. It's up to you all I know is that if you stand by your product you should give one too, it increases buyer confidence and makes your visitors less hesitant to take the plunge and buy from you.

Get That Sale!

You've been spending all your time meticulously aligning all of your bowling pins in a perfect triangular formation, now it's time to hit a strike. You've lead them all this way from beginning to end, you've removed their doubts and objections, calmed their fears and left no question unanswered, now it's time to get the sale.

How do you get the sale?

You ask for it.

If it's not clear what you want your prospect to do they'll be wandering in the aimlessly until they leave your site even if they've come all that way. Make it clear and ask for the sale. Tell them how to buy, lead them to the order button. Tell them they can receive their product just minutes from ordering no matter what time of day or night.

Bonuses Done Right

Add bonuses to your sales copy to seal the deal. Make sure they're related and compliment your offer. As an example if you were selling an ebook on bass fishing techniques you could include a bonus on choosing the perfect lure for bass fish. It's targeted to your offer and adds value; it's enticing to your prospects and gives them an even stronger reason to buy.

Too often I see people peddling the same old rehashed, completely unrelated products just to make the sale but this can do more harm than good. It gives the impression that you need them to sell your product and that your product can't stand alone to be sold in its own right. Your prospects will question the quality of your product if you need a whole bunch of old bonus products to sell it with. Bottom line, only include them if they make sense and add value to your offer and drive you closer, not further from the sale.

To PS or Not To PS

I always use a PS. It just brings it home. It's the final icing on the cake that gets them to act. It sums up everything they've read from your sales letter and why they should order from you now.

You'll be amazed that some of your prospects will even read to the bottom of your page, right up to the very last character when it comes to making up their mind.

The PS is really for them, if your benefits and guarantee haven't quite sold them yet then your PS and PPS are your safety net.

So make your PS as good as the rest of your sales copy. Trust me, people will read them.

Scarcity and Time Limits – How Not To Do It

Limiting your offer or raising your current price in the near future will increase sales. This creates fear from loss and motivates your prospects to buy on the spot.

However, avoid those cheesy countdown scripts that never reach 0. This will hurt your credibility if you claim your offer will expire forever in 90 minutes only for your prospect to refresh the page and the 90 minutes starts all over again.

If you want to play the scarcity card, mean it. Offer only x amount of product before you pull your offer and then do it, no exceptions. It will give you instant credibility and your prospects will be quick to jump on your offer the next time around.

If you're going to pull an offer after x amount of time then get a proper script that will disable the ability to order just to show you mean business. Everything reinforces your credibility and that you are a person of your word. People will appreciate and respect you for that.

End Note:

Practice makes perfect when it comes to copywriting you get better at it with time. Just make sure you speak to your prospect like they're the only one in the world, you want to connect with them so keep your language plain, answer their questions, remove their objections, fulfill your promises and give them what you promised and more.

From my observation the most popular sales copies are the ones that follow a format, headline, bold statement, story, benefits, features, remove objections, guarantee, and call to action.

I also find that the look of the ad copy mimics old school copy taken from direct marketing. Most web pages look like they come straight out of newsprint, the kinds of ads you would expect to find in a magazine or newspaper this is because we were conditioned to receiving ads in this format during the days of offline direct marketing.

Because we recognize and respond to this format it's still being used today, and for good reason because it still works. No matter how times have changed we still respond to the same things, fear, love, vanity, security, we as people are still the same.

...and don't forget to spell check. Having too many errors can make your sales copy look unprofessional and amateurish.

If you want to learn more about great copywriting technique then I would definitely recommend you search out the best in the business:-

• Gary Halbert
• Yanik Silver
• Jay Abraham
• Clayton Makepeace
• Michael Fortin
• Ted Nicholas
• Joe Sugarman

Here's another site you should look at http://www.hardtofindads.com

This site captures the best display, direct marketing ads you used to find in the magazines growing up. Expand your copywriting education even further and borrow from these time tested proven ads with special attention to the top 10.

Here is a template for your ad copy. This gives you a basic foundation to build from. Go back and read the previous pages about copywriting and plug it into your template. Don't be afraid to make mistakes you can always hit the backspace button.

I've also included a web template for you in the resell package you purchased to substitute your own ad copy directly into. Once you've completed it, you can upload it to the web and sell directly from it.

Sample Sales Letter Template

Put Your Attention Grabbing Headline Here, You've Got 3 Seconds To Make It Count!

Important sub headline that goes into more detail from your headline and encourages visitors to read more.

Question 1 - ask reader questions addressing a frustration to relate to them

Question 2 - another question addressing another frustration

Question 3 - third and final question to the reader

Well, if you answered "Yes!" to any of these questions then you need (Your Product Here)

Introduction going to into more depth about your product, talk for a paragraph or more.

If you've tried other products in the past that just haven't worked for you...

The problem with these other products, diets, services, fill in the blanks

Problem with other products is.....

It's Really NOT Your Fault

Now you have at your fingertips the thing that will help you lose the weight, catch bigger fish, save the time, look better, feel better, increase the confidence, increase your income, double your business productivity, give you more freedom because your product is the answer they've been looking for. Your product should help them avoid pain and to bring them pleasure.

With your product your prospects can expect

☑ **Feature One/Benefit One**

☑ **Feature Two/Benefit Two**

☑ **Feature Three/Benefit Three**

☑ **Feature Four/Benefit Four**

☑ **Benefit Five/Feature Five**

☑ **Feature Six/Benefit Six**

☑ **Feature Seven/Benefit Seven**

All The Tools You Will Ever Need To Succeed This Time

If you've been struggling for a long time and have poured endless dollars down the drain looking for solutions **(Your Product)** is exactly what you need.

Stop wasting your money, your search for answers ends today.

When you secure your copy of **(Your Product Name Here)**

Here's what you'll discover:

☑ Fact One
☑ Fact Two
☑ Fact Three
☑ Fact Four
☑ Fact Five
☑ Fact Six
☑ Fact Seven
...and lots, lots more

Would you really like to know how to solve your problems for good this time?

I understand where you are. It's normal to have a healthy dose of scepticism and so you should.

It's because of this that I want to completely eliminate all of your doubt and put your mind at ease.

This is why I have decided to offer you a money-back guarantee.

This Program Will Work For Or You Get Your Money Back

If for any reason you aren't satisfied at all just send me an email letting me know and I will refund every last penny of your purchase.

Did I mention that you also have a full 60 DAYS to make up your mind too?! You get to give Your Product Name Here a really good going over for 2 WHOLE MONTHS before you ever have to make a decision, no catches.

You can't ask for more than that.

<u>Get Started Right Now!</u>

Special Price

Save $xx.00
~~Not~~ $xx

Only
$XX

Where do you see yourself in 6 months from now? Healthier?, happier?, slimmer?, more freedom?, richer?, increased confidence?, clearer skin?, happier relationship?, with your perfect mate?, smoke free?

If you do, this is what you have been looking for, finally the answer to your questions to change your life for good this time. You don't have to be overweight anymore, you get to make that choice.

Your Product Name Here is available at your fingertips, ready to start when you are. To change your life, all you have to do is click on the order button below to get your copy now, no matter what time of day. You can be reading this in as little as 3 minutes from now, it's that easy.

You can't afford to miss this opportunity, so don't delay.

The only regret you'll have is not finding this sooner.
P.S. Strong reason to close the deal.

P.S.S. Reminder of the risk removal and the 60 day money back guarantee.

You will have in your hands all of the tools you need to finally achieve the freedom, the weight loss, the perfect mate, fill in the blank and for all or you won't be out of pocket a single penny.

GUARANTEE: Get your copy of "**Your Product Here**" right now and read it over. Try the information out. If you are for any reason at all not 100% satisfied, send me an email within 60 days after purchasing, and I will personally refund every penny of your money, no questions asked. It's as simple as that.

To Your Success,

Your Name
Your Website
Your Email

If You Don't Want To Write Your Own Sales Copy

You know me I always give alternatives. If writing your own ad copy seems a little overwhelming at the beginning you can always outsource the task.

Here is someone that I recommend. He has a site that offers unlimited sales copy letters for $97/month. To have a professional copyrighter create you a sales page usually cost from $297 to $10,000. So his prices are very reasonable. www.nolimit-copy.com and his results are proven.

Again, another place that is frequented by world class copyrighters is the War-rior forum. Just as with the ghost writers you can contact the copyrighters with any questions you have as well as check out their testimonials from past clients.

Now that we've covered everything about your resell product development down to re-writing and outsourcing your product creation to production and distribution even to the finer points on writing your crucial sales copy, it's now time to think about your graphics.

Graphics – Everything You Need To Know

Nothing injects new blood into your products quicker than a facelift with a brand new graphic.

Your graphics should relate to your product. I try to make mine a little fun and quirky so that it gets my prospects attention and stands out in their mind. You want your prospects to know what they're getting so it makes sense to use an image related to your product. Your e-cover graphic should sum up your product so that if you knew nothing about the product at all your ebook cover should explain it.

Because this ebook is about revamping old resell rights products for profit I emphasized the age of resell products with cobwebs and spiders.

How important are your graphics? They are your store window, this is what people browse before they decide to check out your products in further detail.

A picture really is worth a thousand words so it's important to use top notch graphics especially when it comes to building a perception of quality. Not only that but a solid good quality graphic gives what your selling credibility. It represents a tangible real world product, the kind your customers would expect to physically pull off the shelves at Barnes and Nobles.

Did you know that a good quality graphic can boost your sales by as much as 300%? So it's worth doing right. Poor quality graphics give the illusion of a poor quality product, remember your graphic is your storefront.

Do It Yourself

I think it's great to have a go at creating your own graphics in the beginning. It saves you money and gets you acquainted with the elements of good design. You have the added advantage of being clear in what you want when the times comes for you to outsource.

The first place to begin is with your images. Images are the lifeblood of your e-covers. Before you go out collecting images everywhere on the internet you must make sure that you are aware of the terms of use. To download any image for the purpose to use in its current form or for alteration without knowing the rights for use of that image could land you in some hot water.

Here are some things you can do:

You can purchase royalty free graphics packages from the internet, most of them have been around for ages but at least there are no copyright restrictions placed on these particular graphics. The developer created and compiled these graphics with that in mind so you are free to use them in any way you wish. With a little creative imagination you can revamp, re-arrange and alter them to look brand new. You can purchase packs with hundreds of graphics for just dollars so you're not short on choice.

Here's a decent looking pack I found http://www.graphicspak.com

You will own the rights to these which means that you can do pretty much anything you want with them.

You can also go to your local stationary store and buy royalty free graphics CD's, a similar concept as the graphics packs.

You can also approach artists from picture sharing sites such as flickr.com for permission to use their graphics. There are some artists who have submitted their work under the creative commons license which stipulates that you can use their images under certain conditions, for example you can use images for your graphics as long as you give the artist credit.

Always make sure that you adhere to this. If you find a graphic that you like for your e-covers ask the artist for permission to use it or if you can, offer to buy it.

There are several top quality sites that carry their own stock of professional images. These are the work of photographers. The majority of pictures that you see on professional websites are from image stock sites like these.

http://www.sxc.hu/browse.phtml?f=search&txt=business&w=1&x=0&y=0

Some of the graphics have been kindly donated by artists. You are permitted to download some of the graphics for free but you first must check the terms and conditions of use and let the artist know you would like to use their work in exchange for credit by way of a thank you and acknowledgment on your site. A fair trade for some top quality graphics.

Here are some more image stock sites:

http://www.fotosearch.com
http://www.bigstockphoto.com
http://pro.corbis.com

www.istockphoto.com is a very popular one. You can get great graphics for as low as $1 each. There are several categories of stock photos to choose from, i.e. business, health, dating, environmental, childcare, etc.

There are however terms and conditions that you have to be aware of.

You can use the images for your own personal business. That means that you can use it for your own website or the websites of your clients if you are a web designer.

What you cannot do is to use these graphics if you intend to resell them as these image stock companies see this as a violation of their terms and conditions. This is because when you resell images you are in effect in direct competition with these image stock companies or this is at least how they see it.

What I recommend is that you start with the graphics packs and CD's, when creating resell rights products that you are giving others the right to resell.

Later on when you earn some good money you could then pay extra for an extended license, this allows you to resell these graphics in the form of your web templates and e-covers to your customers.

Image Terms and Conditions

Once you make some decent money and you want to use istockphoto's graphics for your ecovers and templates then you might want to go for the extended license for electronic items for resale or other distribution- unlimited run. This allows you to resell your graphics using istockphoto's images an unlimited number of times so that your sales volume is in no way restricted.

From istockphoto:

You may also purchase the option to resell the Content in an unlimited number of electronic templates for e-greeting or similar cards, electronic templates for web or applications development, PowerPoint or Keynote templates, screensavers, and email or brochure templates.

Extended License Options	Images & Illustrations	Videos
Unlimited Reproduction / Print Runs	125 credits	150 credits
Multi-Seat License: unlimited users	75 credits	100 credits
Items for Resale (limited run)	125 credits per option	N/A
Electronic Items for Resale (unlimited run)	125 credits	150 credits

Electronic Items for Resale or Other Distribution - Unlimited Run

Notwithstanding the restriction contained in section 4(a) of the Standard License Prohibitions prohibiting the use or display of the Content in items for resale, you shall be entitled with respect to this specific Content to produce an unlimited number of the following items for resale, license or other distribution:

A. electronic templates for e-greeting or similar cards, electronic templates for web or applications development, PowerPoint or Keynote templates, screensavers, and email or brochure templates in or on which the Content is used or displayed (the "E-Resale Merchandise"), provided that:

   i. the right to produce the E-Resale Merchandise in no way grants any rights to you or any recipient of the E-Resale Merchandise in any intellectual property or other rights to the Content;

   ii. you agree to indemnify the iStockphoto Parties from any cost, liability, damages or expense incurred by any of them relating to or in connection with any of the E-Resale Merchandise;

   iii. all other terms and conditions of the Agreement remain in full force and effect, including all Prohibited Uses.

But hey, if you want to really think out the side the box, there are some cool e-covers that are just black with some nice fancy text which can be just as effective. I've seen some sleek, clean looking covers that are all white with just text that grabs your eye.

Here's a magazine cover I made without the use of any graphics, only color and text, I don't know about you but I think it does the trick.

So it's up to you, feel free to use images or not. I'm just showing you that you have several choices.

Now that we've got our images or have opted to go plain, we can start creating our e-cover.

Not All Graphics Software Is Created Equal

What do you think?

It's true that people judge a book by its cover and e-covers are no different. Which looks more professional to you? Which one would you be more likely to buy?

The first image was created with a low end ebook creator software that you can find floating around on the internet for free.

You don't have control over your graphics when you use this type of software. You're stuck with whatever size e-cover the software generates for you and if you enlarge your graphics you lose image quality and the graphic becomes blurred.

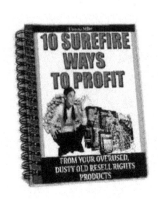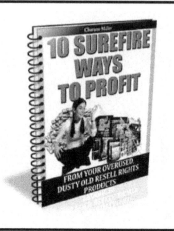

The image on the right I created using a software application called Cover Action Pro www.coveractionpro.com it's a reasonably priced software package that works in conjunction with Photoshop. You need CS or higher for this to work and it's not compatible with Photoshop elements. It works on both Windows and Mac user platforms.

All you do is purchase the program for $97 (you earn your money back in no time) and it installs action scripts that will be added to Photoshop. You create your design based upon their templates, click a button and the script magically twists and folds the pixels into a stunning looking e-cover. You're not just limited to e-covers either but you get a whole variety of shapes like boxes, CD and DVD covers, membership site cards, etc.

It's easy to use and only took 2 hours to create, including the graphic design. If your need some design inspiration they also have some pre-created templates that you can use to get started quicker.

Just to show you the realism of the graphics I created an e-cover like the ones on magazines.com only I made it into a 3D magazine cover, the kind you would expect to pull off the shelves from your local magazine shop. This is important because it represents a real product to your prospect and people like to see what they get.

The graphics are 300dpi which means sharper quality and clarity, no matter how much you enlarge the image the resolution loss is minimal.

300dpi is good because it's the maximum quality image you can have without it being too big.

Tutorials:

http://www.youtube.com/watch?v=SbczvgNCBU4&feature=related

If you have access to Photoshop there are some amazing, free tutorials that I have used to teach myself. You can learn anything from creating incredible ebook covers to eye grabbing software packages. If you want to get really artsy they have the inside tips of the pro's which you can get here: http://www.tutorialized.com

Another tutorial site: http://www.pixel2life.com

E cover tutorial:

http://www.youtube.com/watch?v=ZsamSEiwkm0&feature=related

Because Photoshop can be quite expensive an alternative is the less expensive Photoshop elements. This is a lesser version of Photoshop yet enough to create some stunning graphics with. Remember that Photoshop elements is not compatible with Coveraction Pro should you wish to use it for creating your e-covers with.

Always use jpeg images for the web as they are smaller in size to bitmaps and they load much quicker on the page.

Creating Your Own Ebook Covers Without Photoshop

http://www.jasonscrazydeals.com/web20covers/

http://www.ecover-go.com

http://www.ecoverswithoutphotoshop.com/

A free alternative to Photoshop and a much user friendly program is GIMP (GNU Image Manipulation Program).

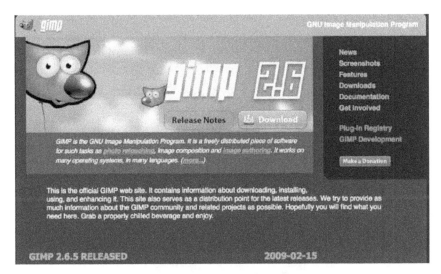

http://www.gimp.org

You download the software which gives you the ability to create your own graphics and e-covers. It's fully functional and can be used by both professionals and newbie's. The software has several powerful features which allow you to refine your graphics like the pro's do no matter what skill level.

Here are some tutorials that walk you through how to make nice looking e-covers for free using GIMP.

http://www.youtube.com/watch?v=e9KD7TvfXFw&feature=related

http://showmedo.com/videos/video?name=2820000&fromSeriesID=282

Another good one is www.paint.net. This produces some fine e-covers too and is pretty straightforward to use.

Here's another of my favorite e-cover creator software and the image that I made using it. This is from the team at Laughingbird. Their software allows you to create logos, web graphics, headers, banners and of course e-covers in all sizes and resolutions.

http://www.webgraphicscreator.com

Works for both Windows and Mac. Once downloaded and installed the software provides a one stop shop taking you from the design phase all the way through to the completion of your e-cover without the use of Photoshop. It's very user friendly and you're able to easily move and manipulate layers by simply clicking and dragging the image you're working on. I wished Photoshop had that feature.

Another great ecover action script software program.

http://www.ecoverpro.com/ecover.html

Tutorial:

http://www.youtube.com/watch?v=s7TA71Cw1FQ

What type of graphic to use?

Ok, because people are so accustomed to buying real books in the real world they expect to get what they order.

For example some people equate large text book type e-cover graphics with getting a long ebook with 200 plus pages. It's what they expect.

So what do you use?

For ebook's 49 pages in length and under you can use the "Magazine" style graphic.	
For ebook's 50 to 149 pages in length you can use the "Binder" style graphic.	
For ebook's 150 pages in length and over you can use the "Book" style graphic because it's true people expect to receive what they see.	

Just remember people expect to get what they see, if they see a thick text book graphic and yet they only receive a 30 page ebook even if it's worth the money they will feel a little ripped off, it's a well known fact, so give them what they expect and include a graphic that accurately sums up the size of the content on offer.

To really get inspiration for your ecovers take a look at some real book covers from the library and bookstores. Amazon.com is another good one. Anything that resembles a real book cover works well and adds credibility to your product.

Play around with colors and fonts. You'll be amazed that an effective looking ebook cover is little more than some nice looking font and plain, clean colors.

When you create your ebook covers don't' forget to make them different sizes:

E-cover Graphic Size	Width (pixels)	Height (pixels)
250	250	278
300	300	333
400	400	444

Don't beat yourself up on getting it perfect either. A less than perfect e-cover is much better than no e-cover at all.

What If Graphics Aren't Your Cup Of Tea?

No problemo. Maybe graphics are a little overwhelming for you or maybe you don't have the time then outsourcing might be for you. It's incredible what graphic designers can produce in a matter of a few short days and at reasonable prices too.

Here are some fantastic companies that do great work in minimum time and at very fair prices. You just need to check out their portfolios and testimonial's from satisfied customers to see what I mean.

www.coverscorp.com
www.ecoverartist.com
www.graphicsgenie.com
www.graphicsalien.com
http://www.extremewebgraphix.com

Making It Easy For Your Customers

Now that you have your e-cover completed you will have a clear idea on how proceed with your sales page template. Just like what you would have received in your resell rights product package, an index.html or a sales.html file you are going to create your own web template to include in your package so that your customers can resell your product to others or upload that template to sell the product themselves.

People like things readily made, it means that at the drop of a hat they can start selling your product immediately and that it's ready to go. This is why including a template complete with sales copy is so important it also makes your resell rights product even more valuable that you'll be able to charge for more it.

Take a breath, the hard part is already done. The product is created, the sales page written, the e-cover completed. All you need to do now is use the same color scheme and theme for your sales template. You can outsource this, in fact those graphic designers I shared with you earlier create web templates in addition to e-covers all the time, it's part of their business so it's no problem for them to do both for you.

If you want to do it yourself I am enclosing a readymade template for you to alter and use as your own. All you need to do is to load it to an html editor like WYSIWYG (What You See Is What You Get), Xsitepro or even Mozilla which is completely free.

You can grab Mozilla from here:

www.mozilla.org

Install Mozilla Open "Composer".

Click open and load the index.html template I've given you. To do this find the location where you saved the index.html file. This could be on your desktop or in your download's folder.

I would also give your sales page a title, this is what will display when it's live on the web. Click on the <HTML> Source tab on the bottom left hand corner of the screen.

Don't freak out that it's in html code. This is super easy. You're going to re-name your page so that your customers will see it online and know what your page is about.

If you're selling bass fishing techniques you might want to name your page "The Hottest Bass Fishing Techniques". Near the top of the page you will find the html code:

```
<meta name="keywords"
content=" keyword1, keyword2, keyword3, keyword4, keyword5">
<title>Your Website Name Here</title>
```

Simply replace Your Web Site Name Here with your site name.

```
<title>The Hottest Bass Fishing Techniques</title>
```

Click on the "Normal" tab, on the bottom left hand side of the screen.

Then click "Save". Then click on "Browse" in the tool bar on the top of the page and will show how your page will look once uploaded the internet.

Your web site name should be displaying on the uppermost top left hand corner.

Now we're going to add our keywords, that great thing is that we've already done our research so all that's left to do is plug our keywords right into our meta tags, this is so that our prospects can find us when searching for on Google.

Go back to your html source by clicking on the <HMTL> Source tab like we did before. This time instead of altering the page title we're going to add keywords.

```
<html>
<head>
  <meta http-equiv="content-type"
  content="text/html; charset=ISO-8859-1">
  <meta name="keywords"
  content=" keyword1, keyword2, keyword3, keyword4, keyword5">
  <title>Hottest Bass Fishing Techniques</title>
```

Just replace each keyword with your own relevant keywords that describe your product. Use some of the keywords you would have found while researching, for example: bass, bass fishing techniques, lures, crappie, crappie bait, etc.

```
  <meta http-equiv="content-type"
  content="text/html; charset=ISO-8859-1">
  <meta name="keywords"
  content="bass, bass fishing techniques, lures, crappie, crappie bait">
  <title>Hottest Bass Fishing Techniques</title>
```

Once you've added the keywords that will help your prospects find you then click the "Normal" tab and then "Save" and there you have it. You'll show up on the search engines every time someone searches for those terms. Because we did our research it will be easy for your prospect to find you because we targeted low competition keyword phrases allowing us to rank highly for our chosen keywords.

All you do is fill in the blanks of your template, click "Save" then "Browse" to preview it and you've got a readymade sales letter ready to roll out.

Once you know how to do there is no limit to the number of websites and web pages you can create. The more of these you can create the more you add to your money making machine.

Being able to do this yourself can save money and there's no limit to the number you can create. This is basic web design as its best, you will get faster and better as time goes on. When you start earning more money on a regular basis with your resell rights products then you can outsource more and more as you go.

If you want to fully outsource your graphics straight out of the gate then feel free to check out the web designers I shared with you earlier, they do a fantastic job.

Adding Your Own Graphics To Your Website Template

Open your web template in Mozilla. Alter your content by filling in the blanks then find a place on your website template that you would like to include your ebook graphic, then:

Get Started Right Now!

Special Price

Save $xx.oo
~~Not $xx~~

Only $XX

☑ **YES!** (YOUR NAME), I can't wait to get my copy of (YOUR PRODUCT)!

I'm Clicking the Button Below and Ordering Right Now!

Go to the toolbar at the top of the page and click on the "Image" Icon.

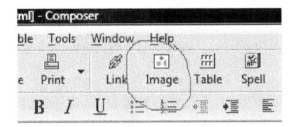

Click on the "Choose File" button.

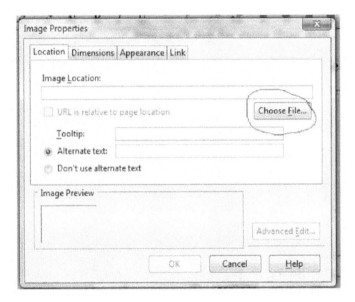

Now you're going to browse for your image to add to your web template. Either

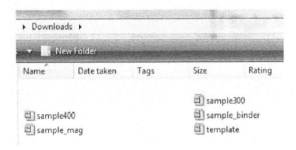

look on your desktop or in your documents or downloads folder.

Choose your image then click "Open".

The following box will open up with your image in the Image Location box. What you need to do is remove the location extension at the beginning of your image file. This is to avoid issues when it comes time to upload your image file to the internet. If you don't remove the extension when you upload it to the net it won't be able to display the file because it will try to reference it to your desktop location when what we need is for it to be independent of its location.

For example: /Downloads/sample300.jpg we need to delete the /Downloads/ portion and leave just the sample300.jpg part.

Select the "Don't use alternative text" then click "OK".

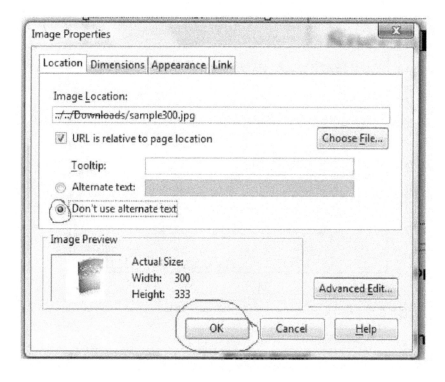

Special Price

Save $xx.00
~~Not $xx~~

Only $XX

There you have your image. This is a great skill to have because it means that you can add any image to your website from now on.

Bonuses Revisited

Are there any other bonuses you would like to add?

I mentioned before, bonuses like graphics also reflect the quality of your offer. Don't feel you have to throw in stale old crusty bonuses for the sake of attracting more buyers to your product. You've come this far the is that you want to ruin it with rundown old bonuses. Despite what you may think old bonuses will hurt rather than help your sales.

If you don't have anything related or relevant you can throw in, don't throw in any bonuses at all. Your product will speak for itself.

If you want to add bonuses then why not outsource a few related articles or write some yourself. Again if your resell rights product is about bass fishing techniques, based upon your keyword research you did earlier on you can outsource 5 to 10 articles to one of your capable writers. They can professionally write articles that can be re-sold or edited and used as blog and website content and even articles for submission to directories. I would stipulate in your reseller's license that they can submit to article directories provided only that they alter the content.

This may seem like a lot to do and that there is cost associated with it whether it is time or money but it pays off, any money you make can be used to further grow and automate your business.

Ok, so we've got a product, sales template complete with sales copy, e-cover now we have to price our product. What's it worth? How much are people paying for your information?

Properly Pricing Your Product for Maximum Profit

This can be a tough one. It's like balancing on a tightrope. You want to offer the types of rights that will be the most appealing without completing pricing yourself out of the market but then you don't want to sell yourself short either leaving profits on the table.

If you offer personal rights it's only good for individual use. If a person purchases your product it is for their individual use only, they cannot resell the product on for profit.

If you offer unrestricted resell rights these are the most powerful rights however because they are unrestricted there is no control over how they are used.

The downside is that because there are no restrictions some people price so low they essentially devalue them which is how you probably came across those $1 resell rights packages in the first place. Try to strike up a balance between giving people enough flexibility with the rights that they are able to profit from them without them selling them too cheaply spoiling for the others that purchased your product.

This is something that you're going to have to ultimately test for yourself but I would start out with Master Resell rights. That way people get to make money with it but with certain restrictions that will make it profitable for everyone and preserve the integrity of your product.

Try 2 different price points for flexibility. Sell it for $17 for personal rights and $37 to $47 for Master Resell rights. Give them a choice and that way you're satisfying both sets of customers, those who genuinely want your information and those who want to make money with your opportunity.

Always experiment with your price point, you will get it down to a fine art with a little testing that you will almost instinctively know what people are willing to pay.

I would say that you're almost ready to sell your product. You've done well, you've learnt lots and now you've picked up new skills that will explode your business in massive proportions.

Putting All
The Pieces Together

Now that we've created the product, wrote the sales copy, created the graphics now all that's left to do is create a website to sell your product from.

You've already got the web template, after all in essence that's all a website really is is just a single page template uploaded to your hosting company's server. That's the only difference between a web page and a template.

You need a simple website for your business so that your customers can find you and order from you. You can get a domain name and hosting for just $7.95/month. I use www.bluehost.com their support is fantastic, you get unlimited storage space and unlimited bandwidth.

This means that you have a heavy duty hosting service to really grow your business. If you decide to offer downloads from your website in future, no matter how many of your customers download and use your bandwidth you never pay extra for it. Some companies charge you by the MB once your limited is reached which can really add up but not bluehost.com.

I have several sites with them and their online support is second to none. You pay the yearly fee upfront so you never have to worry about monthly billing for your hosting with the added bonus that you can host unlimited domain names using the same hosting account. That means that you pay the $96 fee only once a year for all the hosting you want.

After you pay once for your hosting for the year you can create additional websites by paying just $10 for each domain name you register with bluehost.com. This time you register from your back office so that you don't pay for hosting again, you upload your new domain to your existing bluehost.com hosting account. Apart from paying just once a year you never have to worry about monthly hosting fees no matter how many sites you have. Pretty neat, huh?

Some other great hosting sites are: www.hostgator.com, www.dreamhost.com, www.monsterhost.net which pretty much offers the same thing as www.bluehost.com. I know that www.hostgator.com allows you to create a reseller account so that if you want to flip websites you can still bill the customer if they choose to keep their hosting with you which makes for a nice passive income.

When choosing your domain name make it relevant to your product. This is where our research and keywords really kicks in.

For example if people are searching on the phrases "best bass fishing techniques" then it would make sense to name your domain that. www.bestbassfishingtechniques.com. If the domain name you want is not available keep trying different combinations of keyword search terms until you get one that is. This helps your prospects to find you when performing an internet search.

I notice that www.bestbassfishingtechniques.com is already taken but get this, www.topbassfishingtechniques.com is still available. It's a great search term because the combinations of keywords people are searching on are grouped together in the exact order they're searching on which jumps out at them.

You can search for your domain name here:

http://www.bluehost.com/cgi-bin/signup

Just remember you don't have to create a fishing product, I'm just giving you a working example of how it all fits together. You can follow these steps no matter what niche you choose.

When you register your domain name and get your hosting it's very likely they will have cPanel. This is a very user friendly interface you use to upload your template to the internet. This is the process that turns your web template into a real fully functional website viewable to the world.

First we chose our domain name then we check to see if it's available, in this case we'll use www.topbassfishingtechniques.com, we see that's it's still available.

We then get taken to a screen where we are asked to fill in our payment details.

DOMAIN INFORMATION

Domain Name: **topbassfishingtechniques.com**

Domain Registration: **New Client** ☐ **Add Domain Privacy FREE!**.

ACCOUNT INFORMATION

Business Name:	
First Name:	
Last Name:	
Country:	United States ▾
Street Address:	
City:	
State/Province:	Please Select State (REQUIRED) ▾
Zip Code:	
Phone Number:	Use +1 . 888 555 1234 format.
Mobile Number:	
Fax Number:	
Email Address:	This is where your receipt will be sent.

Enter your personal and payment details. You also create your account password when signing up.

You can pay by either credit card or PayPal. Click "Next". After successful payment your site should then be activated within the next 24 hours, usually sooner.

Don't forget to check the email address you used when joining for your receipt which contains your login details, links you can access your site from and the forum and support if you have any questions.

Bluehost.com has 24 hour live online support should you have any questions at all.

Uploading your template to the web is a process known as FTP (File Transfer Protocol) which simply involves transferring your web template and files from your computer to your hosting site making it viewable on the World Wide Web.

Simply go to www.bluehost.com then enter your login details.

After you successfully login you will be taken to your cPanel page. Scroll half-way down the page and you'll the "File Manager" folder. Click it.

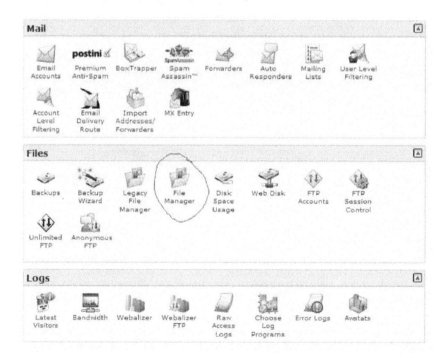

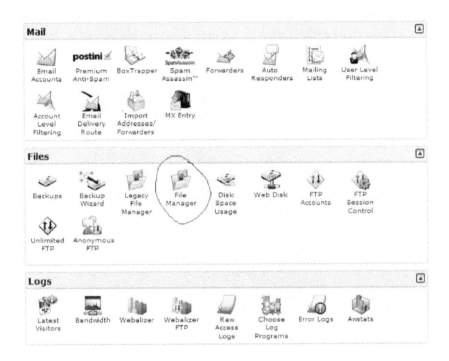

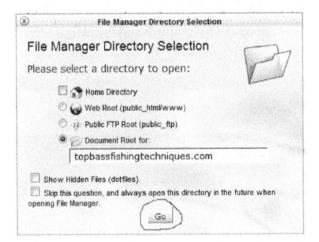

Click on "Go".

Click on the blue earth icon because you're going to open the public html folder to upload your template to. Then click the "Upload" folder icon in the tool bar near the top of the page.

Click "Browse" to upload your template to the web. This prompts you to find where your template is located.

Double click on your file folder to open it up. You can upload each graphic by just clicking on each one.

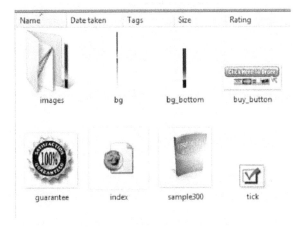

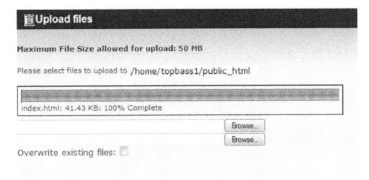

You need to upload your template index.html, your ebook cover image that you created earlier (instructions were given on how to add images to your web template), tick, bg, bg_bottom and guarantee graphics.

You can upload more than one file at a time so upload them all at once.

It's important that you upload your graphics so that they'll appear in your website. Forgetting to upload these will result in broken picture links. As for your buy button, for now we will use E-junkie as a payment processor and we will use their PayPal payment button code.

All you need to do now is enter your URL in your browser bar: www.topbassfishingtechniques.com, click the refresh button and voila, your site is now active on the internet.

Video tutorial of cPanel FTP.

http://www.youtube.com/watch?v=ynmaOLcbW8I

If you need an external FTP client you can use:

www.smartftp.com
http://filezilla-project.org
http://www.ftpclient.org/index.htm

To upload your files only if you're not using cPanel check out this video tutorial:

http://www.youtube.com/watch?v=VROIq95utWs&feature=PlayList&p=6A8FB 034DF2FDF9E&playnext=1&index=17

Collecting Payment

Now that you've got your product completed and your website finished and up-loaded you're going to have to accept payments.

I like to use www.e-junkie.com

They are a 3rd party secure gateway payment processor. For just $5 per month they secure your orders and handle your product delivery for you. There is no bandwidth or transaction limits or transaction fees.

How much you pay each month depends upon how big your products file size is, for example if your products total size comes to 50MB you only pay $5 per month for e-junkie to process and deliver your product. The next size plan up is $10 per month for file sizes of 51 MB to 100MB.

Great value for money especially since your delivery is completely automated for you. When you get into digital products you really want your business to be as automated as possible so that your customers receive their orders instantly without having to wait and without you even having to be there.

Another feature I like about e-junkie.com is that the number of times your product is downloaded is limited which prevents your download link from being shared everywhere. The system usually defaults to a maximum of 5 downloads. You can also set the link to expire within 24 hours.

You can get an idea of the charges per month based upon the following table.

Number of Products	Storage Space (MB)	Can Issue Downloads From Any Server's URL?	Monthly Cost (US$)
10	50	no	$5
20	100	no	$10
20	*	*	$8
40	250	no	$15
60	500	YES	$18
60	*	*	$12
120	500	YES	$27
150	*	*	$16
250	500	YES	$40
350	*	*	$19
500	700	YES	$60
700	*	*	$28
750	900	YES	$90
900	*	*	$40
999	999	YES	$125
1000	*	*	$50
1999	1999	YES	$145
2000	*	*	$100
2999	2999	YES	$165
3999	3999	YES	$185
4000	*	*	$120
4999	4999	YES	$205
5000	*	*	$130
5999	5999	YES	$225
6000	*	*	$140
6999	6999	YES	$245
7000	*	*	$150
7999	7999	YES	$265

We're going to set up your site to accept payments through e-junkie.

First off you need a PayPal account. This is where your money will be deposited after e-junkie successfully processes the order.

If you don't yet have one you can grab one here: www.Paypal.com

If you have an existing PayPal account and you're not already, it pays to get verified.

This means that your business limit, the amount of funds that you can both send and receive is raised. Being verified insures buyer confidence so it's worth getting. What the verification process does is confirm your credit card and postal address and that you are who you say you are.

When you get your PayPal account or have an existing one just get verified by clicking on your "My Accounts" tab and clicking the "Unverified" link and following the instructions.

A small $3 refundable fee will be deducted from your credit card. On your monthly credit card statement will appear the $3 charge along with a PIN number. You simply add this PIN number to verify your details and the $3 fee will automatically be refunded to you. You are now verified.

Open an account in https://www.e-junkie.com/ej/register.php

Log into your account and edit your profile. You need to add your PayPal email address so that e-junkie can link it to your payment button that you use for collecting payment.

SELLING WITH PAYPAL

PayPal Email   sales@topbassfishingtechniques.com

Enter the PayPal email where you will accept payments.

Once you have entered your PayPal email address as well as your other personal details, click "Submit".

Then, click on "Add Product"

To add your product and make it readily deliverable for e-junkie it must be in .zip format. This is so that it compresses the file size to make it smaller which means quicker upload and download times and it also keeps the contents packaged and sent together rather than individually.

It pays to stick to the .zip compression file extension because it is more widely recognized the world over and both Mac and Windows users can easily access it.

Create a new compressed folder on your desktop.

Right mouse click on your desktop, select "New" then scroll down the menu and select "Compress (Zipped) Folder".

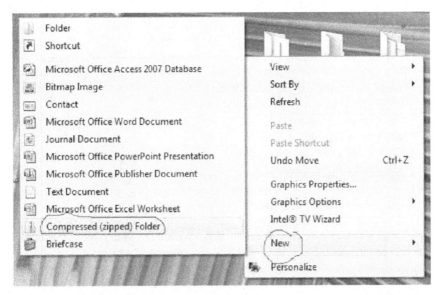

If your product is bass fishing simply call it bassfishing (no spaces) by right mouse clicking on the compressed folders current name and selecting "Rename" and entering bassfishing as your new folder name.

Now you're going to drag and drop everything into your compressed zip folder, from your bass fishing ebook in PDF to your index.html template, to all of the graphics in 3 different sizes including guarantee, tick graphics and any graphics you need to include in your product package.

This is the zipped folder e-junkie will send your customers after they order.

You may also wish to create a PDF for your reseller license as well.

This stipulates what your customers can and cannot do with the product.

Here's an example to use:

[YES] Can edit and put your name on it as the author
[YES] Can sell the Rights
[YES] Can sell the Master Resell Rights
[YES] Can sell The Private Label Rights
[YES] Can sell for whatever price you wish
[YES] Can sell the source code
[YES] Can sell on auction sites
[YES] Can be given away as bonuses
[YES] Can be repackaged
[YES] Can be offered on free membership sites
[YES] Can be offered on paid membership sites

Change it to suit your product, you may not want to give full resell rights or allow it to be offered on free membership sites, you may want to regulate the price in which case you would add:

[NO] Can sell The Private Label Rights
[NO] Can be offered on free membership sites
[NO] Can be sold below the suggested price of $47

Now that our product is ready for adding to e-junkie, we go back to our "Add Product" page.

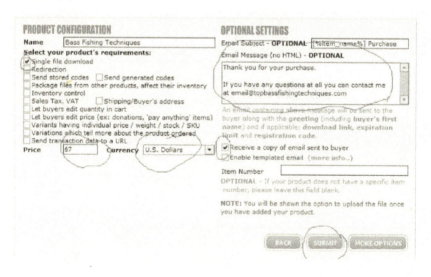

We start with naming your product, in this case it's "Bass Fishing Techniques".

Check the "Single File Download" box. I leave the "Let buyers add quantity in cart" blank because they only ever need to order 1.

Set your price, for this example I've made it $67 and left the currency in "US Dollars".

Next we add an email message thanking your customer for their purchase and adding a contact email that they can reach you should they have any questions.

Check "Receive a copy of email sent to buyer", I always like to know that each customer has received their thank you email with the contact email address in it.

Click "Submit".

Next we click on the "UPLOAD PRODUCT FILE" button.

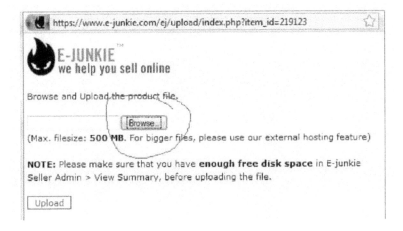

Click "Browse" then locate where your bassfishing compressed zip folder is. If you created it on your desktop that's where you'll find it,

Click it then click "Open" and then "Upload" in e-junkie.

E-JUNKIE™
we help you sell online

Browse and Upload the product file.

| C:\Users | Browse... |

(Max. filesize: **500 MB**. For bigger files, please use our external hosting feature)

NOTE: Please make sure that you have **enough free disk space** in E-junkie Seller Admin > View Summary, before uploading the file.

[Upload]

Please wait while the file uploads.

Uploading

Progress: 8.5%
Speed: 127 Kbps
Estimated time left: 00:16:28

Your product is now uploading into e-junkie's system. The upload time is dependent upon the size of your file.

Once your file is uploaded you need to grab your special PayPal code to accept orders.

Go back to the "Seller Admin" page.

Under "Manage Products" click on "Get BUY NOW/CART buttons for your products"

Your product will come up then click the "GET BUTTON CODE" button.

I usually select the "BUY NOW BUTTONS" tab.

You will see a bunch of html code, this is the code for your "Buy Now" button you are going to paste on your website so that your customers can order from you.

Highlight the code by left mouse clicking and dragging over the code, right mouse click, you should see a drop down box open. Scroll down until you reach "Copy" then left mouse click on it.

Open up your sales letter template in Mozilla and then scroll down to your order button.

We're going to place a word inside your order button that will enable us to properly position where your order button will appear seeing as we're dealing with html code.

The word you use can be any of your choosing as long as it's a word that doesn't appear anywhere else on the page. This makes it easier to find and pinpoint where your code should go.

Let's use the word "Love".

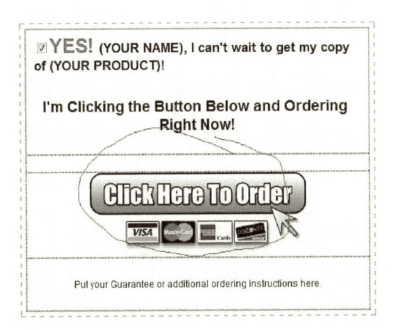

Click on the order button and delete it because we have to replace it with our fully functional e-junkie order button. Then type the word Love in place of the old "Click Here To Order" button.

Then click on the <HTML> Source tab at the bottom left hand corner of the page, this allows you to view to HTML code.

Now we're going to find the word Love and paste our code in its place because we know that's the position we want our order button to be in and this is a much easier way rather than sifting through all of that code and guessing where to place it.

Click CTRL and F, this should open up a search box. Then type in the word Love.

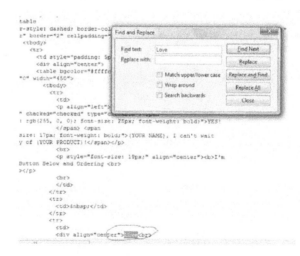

This will then take you to the word which should be highlighted.

Now press "Delete" then press CTRL V to paste your button code.

```
<a href="https://www.e-junkie.com/
```

Click the "Normal" tab on the bottom left hand side of the screen and then click "Save" and then "Browse" to view your button.

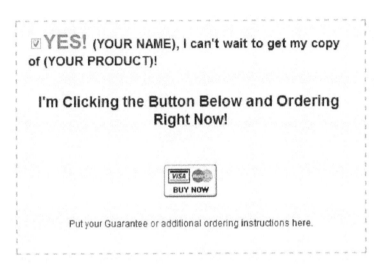

And voila! You have your very own fully fledged order button, linked to your uploaded product and ready to take orders.

This is great to start out with but with time you can eventually move into fancier order buttons by customizing them through PayPal but for the time being this is a great way to start.

You just need to re-upload your index.html (sales template) back up to the web so that your new order button will appear and will be activated.

Congratulations! You made it! You've done all of the ground work that has set you up for maximum success this time. No matter what opportunities that guru's or fly by nighters peddle, this is what it takes to truly be financially independent.

Once you do this a couple of times you will be able to do it with your eyes closed and the power in the skills you've gained will ensure that you make money for the rest of your life with this. I've just chopped weeks and months off of your learning curve and I sure as heck wish I had this when starting out, the majority I learned through massive mistake making and trial and error but not you.

It frustrated me that marketers would assume I already knew how to throw up a website to start selling from immediately and that's where I always came unstuck because my lack of knowledge stopped me right there while at the same time I had information overload in the things I didn't need.

I promise I included everything you need to know and nothing you don't. You follow these steps from beginning to end and you will make a constant, beautiful repeatable income like clockwork.

Ok, thanks for coming this far with me, now it's time to hit this one out of the park.

Now that your product is finished and ready for orders we've got to let people know about it.

11 Traffic Generating Techniques to Drive Floods of Buyers to Your Website

This is where all of the research we did really begins to pay off because knowing exactly what people want and the keywords people are searching under you are now able to get as much targeted free traffic from multiple as you can handle.

Blogs to funnel traffic to your site

To start generating sales you have to let people know about your product, to do that you need to get people to your site.

Remember those keywords that you researched at the beginning?

You are going to use them to start getting traffic to your web page.

Create a blogger blog for free using your keywords in the blog title.

https://www.blogger.com/start

Again if your keywords were bass fishing techniques you would name your blog like this: www.blogspot.com/bassfisingtechniques (if bass fishing techniques isn't already taken). If it is just add top to it and that should do the trick, i.e. www.blogspot.com/topbassfisingtechniques

These are keywords you know people are searching on so when they search for bass fishing techniques your blog will show up.

After you create your blog, write a little about your resell rights product adding a link to your webpage. The idea is to have several of these free blogs funneling traffic to your site to create a passive steady flow of traffic that will continually build over time until it snowballs sending you floods of daily traffic.

You can create several blogs targeting different keyword combinations by using them in your blog name. This ensures that you have several traffic generating blogs sending you plenty of frequent visitors.

After you finish writing a little spiel about your product the next thing to do is to ping it. This simply lets the search engines know that your blog is there. Once it's indexed in the search engines you will start to receive a steady flow of traffic to it.

Pinging let's your customers know you're there and since we know they're already looking for what you have your site will start receiving lots of nice free targeted traffic.

You can ping several blog directories in one hit by using:

http://pingomatic.com
http://autopinger.com
http://technorati.com/ping
http://www.pingmyblog.com
http://www.kping.com

This should give you a head start in bringing your blog to the world. Remember the purpose of your blog is to just redirect traffic to your site so don't forget to include links back to your product site.

Squidoo and Hubpages are great social networking sites that have tonnes of daily traffic that you can tap into to get visitors flowing to your website in little time.

Squidoo

http://www.squidoo.com

Squidoo allows users to create content based lenses around whatever topic the creator wishes to write about.

It can be anything from pets to fishing, golfing, sewing, cars, stamp collecting, hairdressing, dating, relationships, fashion, cooking, crochet, car repair, computers, yoga, singing, arts and the list goes on. It can be about anything of interest to the lens creator.

Squidoo is one of the top 500 most visited sites in the world so it pays to get your lens created and out there.

Squidoo has a revenue sharing program where it splits earnings generated from eBay and Amazon.com between authors, charities and itself.

You can set up a lens in less than an hour. Google gives lots of love to these types of sites because again they are popular, this is where the traffic congregates and new content is constantly being added to it therefore Google assigns priority to it. To dip your cup into the Squidoo traffic stream got to: www.squidoo.com and create your first lens.

Take your keywords, in our case bass fishing techniques. This will be the name of our Squidoo lense for example: www.squidoo.com/bassfishingtechniques. Notice how your keywords are in your Squidoo URL like your blogger blog and just like the blog they will show up in the search engines when your customers search on your keywords.

You'll be everywhere that it will be impossible to not generate traffic to your website. Once you have created your lens you simply fill it with information about your product with a link to your web site.

You can also add tags which are your keywords this will help you target the traffic generated by your lens.

Here's a great tutorial to help you get your first lens up and running quickly.

Squidoo Lens Tutorial

http://www.howcast.com/videos/10752-How-To-Make-a-Squidoo-Lens

Once you finish building your lens that's it. You can create more Squidoo lenses or you can create more content and add it your existing lens.

Once your lens is finished you should add an RSS feed link to it. This means that the moment you make any changes to your lens or update the content your readers will know bring them back to your site.

Hubpages

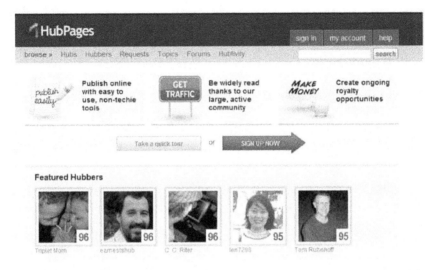

www.hubpages.com

Like Squidoo, Hubpages also encourages user based participation. Anyone can be an author and create Hubpages on any topic they want, the sky is the limit.

Hubpages like Squidoo also has a revenue sharing program with its authors which is primarily generated from Adsense.

Authors are able to create Hubpages around their topics of interest. Placing a link to your website you can use Hubpages as a conduit to drive some decent traffic to your site in little time.

You can get set up with your own Hubpage in just minutes from now by going here: www.hubpages.com

Now we want to start getting that traffic to your Hubpage which will then direct traffic to your website and to your product which we'll achieve by adding tags to your Hubpage. These aren't just any old tags though, these are tags from other Hubpages that experiencing lots of traffic in their own right. If you want to experience the same kind of success for yourself you just have to duplicate what is working for others.

Adding tags to your Hubpage from other high ranking Hubpages allows you to instantly tap into their traffic in as little as an hour. Not bad for going from no web presence to getting a captive audience in hours.

We know we'll get a quick rush of traffic because these "hot" hubs are already generating this massive traffic for themselves and if we have similar tags we can duplicate those results too.

Here's how you do it:

Copy this link http://hubpages.com/tag/yourkeywordshere/hot into your web browser bar and simply replace the "yourkeywordshere" with your own keywords. In our example that would be: http://hubpages.com/tag/bassfishingtechniques/hot of course you would enter whatever keywords your research revealed for your own product.

See which Hubpages come up and then, look through them and find their tags on the right hand side of the screen, simply add similar tags to your own Hubpage so that you can get a piece of that traffic yourself.

A great link to help you get more traffic to your hubpages fast.

http://www.socialmarketingstrategy.com/traffic-and-page-rank-from-hubpages/

Joint Ventures

Find any lists you're currently on that would be interested in your product.

If the email lists you're subscribed to are not a match for your product then you can do a search for any businesses that are. For example if you are selling your bass fishing techniques ebook then you could look for bass fishing or fishing related websites. Look to see if they have any opt in form and subscribe to their newsletter.

After a week or two email the list owner. Don't forget to include that you are a subscriber on their list and what you like about their newsletter or ezine so they know that you are not just mass mailing a bunch of people.

Approach them with your offer, if they are interested give them a copy of your product so they can look over it. Include a description of what your product is about, why it would be beneficial to their subscribers, the price you are selling it for and the business deal you have in mind which is usually 50/50 split.

Be prepared to give away a higher percentage which is fine because you are essentially getting money for free. You didn't have to spend money to get that traffic and you are leveraging someone else's assets which is a fair deal.

You take the sales and simply split it with your joint venture partner for the agreed upon commission percentage.

This is a great way to build a long term business relationship and following your first successful joint venture deal you're bound to get even more deals from the same partner in future.

eBay

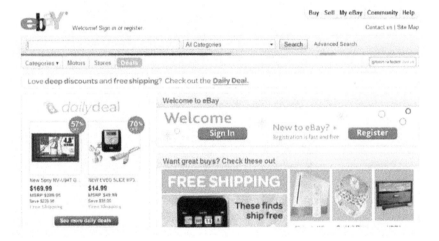

eBay has millions of daily visitors and there are still fortunes to be made there.

There are lots of people that are taking advantage of the "no digital products" policy by selling physical products and are raking in big buck because of it.

To sell on eBay:

1. You can burn your product to CD or DVD and list your auction sell price at $27 or more. That way you can happily auction your products on eBay without violating their terms and services. There are people making a tonne of money this way in fact they use their $17 CD's and DVD's as entry level products for their much higher ticket items. I know of two people that are consistently earn-

ing $15,000 to $30,000 per month on eBay each even during these challenging economic times. So there is money to be made on eBay.

2. The second option if you want to sell your products in digital format is by using classified ads. You pay a once only fee of $9.95 for your ad to be live for a whole 30 days, no extra fees and you have the added advantage of showing in the eBay marketplace alongside the regular auctions as well as showing up in the search engines.

I would do some testing to see if this brings in regular sales then you may want to consider this a permanent fixture of your advertising promotions.

I would also look at placing an opt in box on your web page to your own newsletter so that you can start funneling some traffic and building your own customer list. This means that you are building a long term business with the potential of making a regular ongoing income with your clients. Just make sure that you always offer great quality and keep your information tightly focused on their interests, after all if it's fishing, give them what they expect.

Keep feeding them great information on fishing techniques and every month sell them a product, it could be a mini collection of techniques for catching different types of fish.

When it comes to building your list I would go with Aweber. I'm very happy with their service and you can start for as low as $20 per month. Once your list grows the price goes up by little increments each month but is a small price to pay when you consider the lifetime value of a customer which can be thousands.

http://pages.ebay.com/education/howtosell/index.html

Forums

Depending upon your product just perform a Google search for your targeted forum. If you're looking for fishing forums just search for "fishing forum", "weight loss forum" , "recipe forum", "golf forum", depending upon your niche.

Another great place that we covered in depth earlier in our research was www.bigboards.com which is a collection of several forums under one roof so you are bound to find what you are looking for there.

You can contribute by making regular helpful posts about your niche and by answering member's questions, include the link to your product in your signature file.

This is a great way of getting your prospects attention and an effective way to reach out directly to your target market.

Twitter

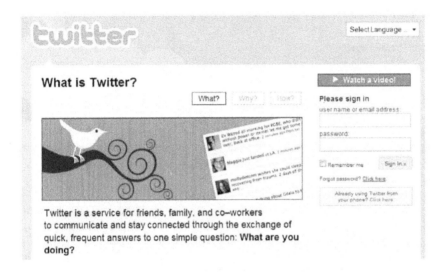

Definition: Twitter is a micro blogging platform which allows you to publish short messages of less than 140 characters through different mediums like IM, cell phones and the web.

What's the big flutter about Twitter these days?

Twitter is a social networking site that allows users to stay in touch with each other the world over in addition to being a great platform to announce your products from.

In the past 6 months Twitter has gained huge popularity and is fast becoming a traffic force to be reckoned with and you can see why.

Twitter boasted 55 million users for the month of February 2009 alone so it's obvious why so many marketers are jumping on the Twitter bandwagon to grab a piece of the Twitter traffic pie.

Join up with Twitter and use it to follow people and to get others to follow you. This will help generate interest in your product and drive even more targeted traffic to your site.

http://twitter.com

Here is a helpful link explaining Twitter in greater depth:

http://tweeternet.com/

Join Twitter and get tweeting today.

By the way, here is a fantastic viral tool that will help drive your traffic through the roof. All you have to do is join Twitter and then add yourself to the system then share it with others. When those that join under you share it with others your product link automatically goes out to all of their people that join under them increasing your traffic exponentially.

You can send it out to your friends to get the ball rolling or create a simple YouTube video with your link at the end in the form of a title so viewers can join under you and help generate traffic to your site. You could also add your link to your signature.

http://tweetergetter.com/

Video sharing sites

To get the most out of video marketing we need to optimize our videos so that our target market will find them.

We do this by creating "tags".

www.tubemogul.com allows you to submit to the top video sites online with the click of a button for free.

The reason why video sites are given so much importance by Google is because they are popular. They generate truckloads of traffic daily and people love to watch video for entertainment and educational purposes. Think about it, video is such a natural medium and because it is part of our daily lives and is something we're well familiar with, it makes sense to use it.

So powerful is video that it's not uncommon to appear on the front page of Google for your keywords within just 24 hours of posting your video when it usually takes weeks for Google to index your website naturally.

In fact just with submitting to video sites, in just one day I received over 2,000 hits to my videos.

So that you rank highly for your keywords use the ones you came up with in your research and use them as your tags for your videos this will ensure that you rank for those search terms scooping up some decent search engine traffic.

Make some videos or slideshows giving valuable information about your product and include a link at the end of your video to your webpage driving some nice, free, targeted traffic to your site.

Video marketing works, give it a go. Tubemogul automates the posting process so that your time is not tied up posting manually.

So create yourself a Tubemogul account and it will show you which video sites it posts to. Register to each of the video sites so that Tubemogul can automate the process for you from that point on.

Some of the top ranking sites are:
1. www.youtube.com
2. www.dailymotion.com
3. www.5min.com
4. www.veoh.com
5. www.metacafe.com
6. www.revver.com
7. www.myspace.com
8. www.howcast.com

How to attract targeted traffic to your website through your videos

Here's a little trick to help you get floods of traffic to your site.

Create your video about product. Make sure that you include a title at the beginning and end of your video for your website URL.

Login to your YouTube.com account.

Upload your video

Click your movie file, in this case it's MyVideo, then click "Open".

Then "Upload Video".

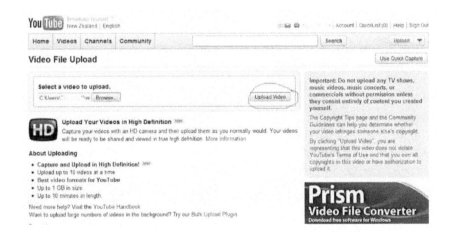

Fill out the video details.

Video File Upload

When entering your **"Title"** for your video, make sure it's relevant to your keywords, this will be the first thing your prospects will see when your video shows up in the search engines.

For your **"Description"** place your website address first then write your video's description after.

This is because when submitting your videos to video sites the only place you can display your website URL is in your actual video in the form of titles. It's great to do this and I recommend it for the extra exposure but it also means that your prospects have to pause on your video and manually type your URL into a browser bar.

This can be time consuming so a great way around this is to include your URL in your description which actually shows up as a clickable link that will take your prospects directly to your site.

So don't forget to add your website URL to your description. Make sure it's the first thing you put for your description which will appear higher up on the page for your prospects to see when viewing on youtube.com

Your **"Tags"** should be your researched keywords, i.e. bass fishing, fishing techniques, fishing lures, etc.

Each time someone searches on these keywords your video will be one of the first things they see.

Select the appropriate **"Category"** from the drop down menu.

Share your video with the world for maximum exposure.

Click **"Save Changes"**.

You're done.

The upload time will vary upon your video size. Once it's live your prospects will be able to find your video and the added bonus is that because you researched low competition, highly targeted keywords you will rank highly on the first or second pages of Google within an hour of your video going live.

Several times after submitting to the top video sites through Tubemogul I've dominated 9 out of 10 search positions on the front page of Google out of 500,000 plus other competing pages, just by doing this alone.

That's truly how powerful video is, take full advantage of it and get making a video today.

Article marketing

Article marketing still works extremely well.

You can outsource the task if you like. Article writing software has given me mixed reactions. I'm yet to find one that can replace a live, breathing human being.

The best thing to do is to either outsource it or write it yourself. You'll be rewarded for providing quality content in the long run.

I'm sure you're well familiar with article marketing, in particular "Bum Marketing" the term coined by article marketing extraordinaire Travis Sago.

The philosophy behind Bum Marketing is that anyone, even a penniless bum off the street can apply the free techniques and make money with them.

Articles are a great way to promote your products because they get indexed quickly by the search engines, Google in particular gives priority to some article directories due to their popularity and the fact that new information is constantly being added to them.

Again all of that keyword research and leg work we did in the beginning really begins to pay off here. Because you didn't just randomly pick any old product from your collection but carefully chose one that had a market and was being searched on you've taken the guesswork out of whether or not you have a product that will sell.

That way you haven't invested all that time and energy creating a product for nothing.

When it comes to writing your articles you can have up to a 2% keyword density. This means that you should not enter your main keyword phrase more than 2% throughout your article content.

For example if your article is 300 words in length you wouldn't want to mention "bass fishing techniques" more than 6 times.

To be honest places like ezinearticles would probably disapprove your articles with that amount. Use your judgment, with ezinearticles I probably wouldn't mention it more than three times at the most throughout the body of your article, use your discretion with other article directories.

Each one varies and it comes down to a matter of trial and error. If you get disapproved, don't worry it happens to all of us, the great thing is that you can do a simple re-edit and re-submit. Just make sure you know why your article was disapproved and make the according changes.

As long as you can strike up that perfect balance between having a decent enough keyword density to get your articles found as well as your article making for a great read then you've got a winning combination satisfying both human and search engine alike.

Because you're clever and you know what people are searching on when it comes to your product, writing your articles with your keywords imbedded throughout them as well as having the same keywords in your article titles will cause your article to rank high on the search pages whenever someone searches on your keywords.

For example if your keywords are bass fishing techniques your article title should reflect this. You would name your article:

**"10 of the Best Ever Bass Fishing Techniques
to Instantly Catch More Fish,
Even If You Are Completely Hopeless"**

See how the keywords are in the title yet we jazzed it up to make it pop to the person searching?

So if a person searched on **"bass fishing techniques"** your article would show up with the keywords highlighted in blue and because the keywords are bunched together in the same order as the person searched the more likely they will click on your link.

Our brains are fascinating creations, they like to group and organize information into chunks. Grouping together the keywords in the same order as they were searched for will give you higher click through rates than if your article title was to look something like this:

**"10 of the Best Techniques Ever For Fishing Bass –
Instantly Catch More Fish,
Even If You Are Completely Hopeless"**

The more relevant you are to what the user is searching for the higher you rank on the search page, for example the first title would outrank the second purely because it was in the same order as the user was searching in.

Structuring your articles this way will ensure that they rank highly and generate plenty of regular, automated traffic that will last for much longer than the quick flood it gets after it's first added to the article directory's high traffic main site.

When submitting your articles another important thing is to add your keywords as meta tags. This will help your article show up in the search engines.

You can grab attention with your headline but don't forget it's the resource box that will get them to your site.

A compelling resource box will get you visitors to your web page. Give them a reason to click through. Maybe your article could be made of two parts where the second part of the article is offered on your site.

You could offer more quality free information. If you give them a good enough reason to click through to your site, they will. Keep testing your resource box. You can edit it to see which one gives you the best results. Once you figure this out then you've cracked the code and can use similar resource boxes with your future offers.

If you can turn out a couple of good articles per day, and it's not difficult to do, you'll be generating a constant stream of traffic for years to come and it cost nothing more than a little time.

If writing is not for you than simply outsource the task to someone else. Give them your keywords to be woven into the content and article title and all you have to do is submit it to the article directories.

Duplicating the article marketing success of others:

What we're going to do is find some of the most articles out there pulling the traffic you want. We just need to find the tags their using to get their articles noticed.

Go to www.ezinearticles.com

To find related articles to your product enter your keyword in the search toolbar. I've entered "bass fishing" to start with, then click "Google Search".

Tips For **Bass Fishing** With CrankBaits

Bass fishing with crankbaits can make going **fishing** very enjoyable. ... When **bass fishing** with crankbaits, there are tips and strategies that you may want ...
ezinearticles.com/?Tips-For-Bass-Fishing-With-CrankBaits&id=1134229 -
Similar pages

Better **Bass Fishing**

If you want to impress your **fishing** buddies on your next **bass fishing** adventure, get this book. ... Swanson, Mary "Better **Bass Fishing**." Better Bass Fishing ...
ezinearticles.com/?Better-Bass-Fishing&id=1950209 - Similar pages

Basic Tips For **Bass Fishing**

Basic Tips For **Bass Fishing**. ... I personally prefer using a light tackle which **fishing** for Bass and would suggest the same. ...
ezinearticles.com/?Basic-Tips-For-Bass-Fishing&id=1934681 - Similar pages

Bass Fishing With Crankbaits - How To Retreive Crankbaits

Bass Fishing With Crankbaits - How To Retreive Crankbaits. ... Dennis has been **fishing** mainly for **bass** for over 45 years. ...
ezinearticles.com/?Bass-Fishing-With-Crankbaits-How-to-Retreive-Crankbaits&id=1100106 -
Similar pages

Best **Bass** Lures - Exploring the Best **Bass Fishing** Lures

As far as **bass fishing** lures are concerned, spinner baits are one of the best. ... This was a small list of all of the **bass fishing** lures available to **bass** ...
ezinearticles.com/?Best-Bass-Lures---Exploring-the-Best-Bass-Fishing-Lures&id=2001125 -
Similar pages

Largemouth **Bass Fishing** at Lake Gaston

Largemouth **Bass Fishing** at Lake Gaston. ... We caught a few of the Strpiers while **fishing** for **bass** on the Lucky Craft crankbait shown below. ...
ezinearticles.com/?Largemouth-Bass-Fishing-at-Lake-Gaston&id=80732 - Similar pages

We'll select "Tips For Bass Fishing With Crank Baits" from the list.

We then get taken to the author's article but what we're really interested in is the top related articles with the most views.

Scroll further down the page.

1. The Best Bait For Fishing
2. Crappie Fishing - The List You Can't Do Without!
3. Fishing With Worms
4. Catch Crappie Fishing Minnows Amazing Method! Crappie Fishing Secret Part 3
5. Early Spring Bass Lures
6. Live Bait Fishing - Tips For Catching More Fish
7. The Universal Crappie Catching Rig - Check Out These Amazing Crappie Fishing Tips!
8. Ice Shelter Basics
9. The Best Bait - Is There a Best Fishing Bait?
10. Using Worms For Fishing - Tips to Be More Successful When Fishing With Worms
11. Special Winter Carp Fishing Tackle and Bait Tips!
12. Worm Fishing - Tips For Successful Angling
13. About Fishing Hooks
14. Bass Fishing 2009
15. How to Rig a Spinner For Trout Fishing

Most Published EzineArticles in the Recreation-and-Sports:Fishing Category

1. Fishing Tackle Equipment - What You Need to Know
2. Those Wily Walleye Fish
3. Want to Catch More Fish? Read on to Find Some Advice on What Bait to Use!
4. Deadly Fish - An Important Read For Every Fisherman!
5. Catch More Fish Now! A Step by Step Guide
6. Ice Fishing in Montreal
7. Dry Fly Fishing the Muskegon River - How to Fish "Big Water"
8. Planning a Fishing Vacation You Won't Forget
9. Spinnerbait Fishing
10. Caught Some Fish? Read on to Find Out the Best Ways to Cook Your Fish
11. Fly Fishing With Streamers on the Muskegon River
12. Crappie Rods & Reels - The Good, Bad & Ugly
13. Stream Trout Fishing
14. Big Carp Fishing Bait - Cold Water Tips!
15. What Everyone Ought to Know About Halibut Fishing

Let's click on "The Best Bait For Fishing".

Scroll down the page. Amazing, so far this article has received 2526 views since Dec 22nd 2008. That's 2526 views in 79 days (11th March 2009 today).

That works out to 32 views per day and 959 views per month. Fantastic considering it's completely free traffic.

Please Rate This Article: ★★★★★ (5 votes, average: 4.4 out of 5)

Let's look at the tags this author is using so that we can use similar ones for ourselves which should help us attract some of that traffic to our articles.

Scroll back up to the top of the page. There you'll find a menu.

Click on "Ezine Publisher"

Scroll down to the bottom of the page until you get to keywords and then use those for your own articles.

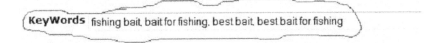

Obviously these keywords have worked well for this author to draw in the massive amounts of article views, all you need to duplicate some of this success for yourself is to copy, modify and add some of your own unique to your product.

Add these keywords when submitting your own articles and also use your keywords that you researched. When you do this your article will show up ranked highly in Google because you have little competition.

Don't forget to include your keywords in your title. Make sure they are tightly focused and grouped together as in our previous example because it visually stands out more to your prospect as being relevant and what they are specifically looking for.

You can use this method for any niche to track down the best keywords for your articles.

Other title buzzwords:

- Greatest
- Best
- Proven
- Time Saving
- Money Saving
- Revolutionary
- Incredible
- Effective
- Really Works
- Revealed
- Guaranteed
- Easy
- Simple
- Quick
- Effortless

"How to" titles and articles with "steps" seem to work quite well.

People love to learn new things and giving it to them in simple digestible steps makes it easy to follow.

Possible article templates just fill in the blanks.

5 Things You Absolutely Must Do If You Want To…..
5 Mistakes To Avoid Making If You Want….
Top 10 Reasons Why You Should…
5 Crucial Steps To Take When ….
6 Ways In Which You Can…..
5 Tips For…..
10 Easy Steps To Succeed In.
7 Steps To Follow When Choosing A Great…..

Some of the best article directories to post your articles to:

- www.Ezinearticles.com
- www.Goarticles.com
- www.Articlealley.com
- www.Articlegarden.com
- www.Webpronews.com
- www.Articledashboard.com

- www.Searchwarp.com
- www.Isnare.com
- www.Buzzle.com
- www.Americanchronicle.com
- www.Ideamarketers.com
- www.ArticleCity.com

Sign up today and follow the instructions each directory provides when submitting articles to their site.

If you want to automate the article submission process then www.articlesender.com and www.isnare.com might be what you're looking for.

Remember how I said earlier about growing a long term business? Because this is such an effective way of generating traffic to your sites you should include a way to add subscribers to your list. Visit www.Aweber.com when you're ready to take your business to the next level.

Extreme Viral Marketing

This is an awesome way to get some quick traffic to your website.

The beauty of viral promotion is that your website goes out to people you would never have otherwise had access to.

With this free software all you have to do is join up, include the link to your website and send out your special page you receive upon joining to others. When they join under you and send out their special page to their contacts your link goes out with it essentially giving you access to people you could never have reached with your own marketing efforts alone. This has global, far reaching potential to quickly put your link in front of thousands the world over.

You can join here: www.freeviral.com

All you have to do is get a few people under you. If you have no contacts or list of your own, to find other people that are searching for traffic you could post a quick video on www.youtube.com or write up some quick articles and send them out to article directories. You could also have a signature link in your forum posts.

Banner Advertising

Just as we mentioned earlier during our research phase, banner advertizing is still alive and well.

Banners used to be big in the late 90's and was an effective method of advertising at the time however it wasn't until the early millennium that marketers found their click through rates were starting to drop.

It was thought that visitors were becoming blind to banners due to their over exposure. Banners were then used a little less as other methods of traffic generation burst onto the scene. Although banners never really went away it's not until recently that they've made a comeback and are being used more often.

I like banner advertising but it can be somewhat of a hit and miss, the hits more than make up for the misses.

If you're still trying to establish your own traffic what better way to get hold of highly targeted traffic then those who already have it.

Do a Google search for your product and see who's ranking high on the search engines. Also look at websites and forums that are related to your product. Make a list and include the name of the website, URL address and the name of the website owner to contact.

Then drop them an email and ask how much they would charge for you to place a banner on their site for a month. Prices can range anywhere from $50 to $200 and up per month depending upon how much traffic they get coming through their site.

This is a great way of getting your product to the right targeted traffic instantly. It does cost so make some sales from your product with the above free traffic generation methods then try your hand at paid banner advertising.

Other People's Thank You Pages

Something I don't see too often is people capitalizing on the traffic from other people's thank you pages. More often than not, even experienced marketers aren't using their own thank you pages properly.

If you're not sure what a thank you page is it's the page that you are re-directed to as soon as you sign up to a newsletter or ezine. On this page, you will usually find a thank you message plus instructions on how to check your inbox and confirm your registration.

Most people leave the default message you are assigned automatically through your auto responder. Some actually customize this message and give you instructions on how to confirm your subscription and how to white list their email address so that your ezine issues won't get filtered into the spam or junk mail folders.

Yet many are not making the most of the potential of this page and it's a shame because the thank you page is actually a prime piece of web real estate.

I'll use an example of how this works:

Think of it this way. The prospects that just joined your newsletter were already interested in what you had to offer to the point where they handed over email address. This means that they're already in the right mindset, they're already pre-qualified for whatever you're offering so long as it's tightly focused to what your newsletter is about.

How do we know this? Because it took a string of complex decisions to even get them to that point.

They've already had to:

1. View your web page
2. Make the decision to take action and click on your link to opt in to   your ezine or newsletter
3. Subscribe (massive action) by giving you their details

So to get to that stage they've had to take some major action. They're already interested in your newsletter content so why wouldn't they be interested in a quality, related, targeted offer.

For example, let's say you offer a free mini report on fishing from your opt in squeeze page, all those interested in downloading your free report first have to sign up to your newsletter to receive it (this allows you to sell to that person again in the future).

Before they get taken to the download page where they can access their free report, they get re-directed to an up sell page or an OTO (One Time Offer page) which would normally be your generic "thank you" page. Instead of letting that page go to waste it now contains your offer. Using this method can increase your sales by up to 3 times than leaving it blank or with the default subscription message.

People have varying opinions on selling this way. Some don't want to bombard their prospects straight out of the gate which is absolutely fine, but I've used this method and it works well.

With this method you're also able to start building a list of quality customers from the beginning and are creating a repeat list of buyers.

So, take that example of using your own "thank you" page and turn your focus toward using "other people's thank you pages".

This is a similar situation to creating joint ventures but rather than being promoted to someone else's list you are being promoted on their thank you page.

How to find business owners who are already getting the traffic you want?

Find similar business owners related to your field by Google searching them.

Check out their website to see if they have an opt in feature, this means that if they are accepting subscribers to their newsletter than they probably have a "thank you" page as well.

Join their newsletter

Check out their thank you page once you've opted in to their newsletter, if it's generic or has a simple thank you message with signup instructions, include them on your list of people to approach.

If they're already offering up sells on this page, then this is great too because you won't have to spend time explaining the benefits of it to them.

Maybe you can offer to display your ad on their page for a fee, or negotiate a percentage for each sale generated from their site. 50/50 works very well.

Even though you're giving away money upfront it's also money you made from traffic you didn't have to break a sweat getting. You're making the most of someone else's traffic while at the same time creating a mutually beneficial arrangement for the pair of you.

Wait a couple of weeks before you decide to approach, read all of the incoming newsletters they send, do your research. What's topical in the content they present you with? What were the last 3 newsletters about and was there anything that stood out to you about them at all? You're doing your due diligence, gathering your research by getting to know them personally so that when you do approach them, you've done your homework and they'll know it.

When you decide to make contact, tailor your letter to each individual situation. Don't be a bull in a China shop and write one letter for all then mass blast it. Personalize it. Prove that you really are on their list. Make a comment on one of their newsletter posts to show you are paying attention. Paying close attention to detail will pay off in the long run.

Do this a few times before you even approach them with your offer. Build a relationship of trust first then you greatly increase your chances of striking up a deal.

I'm sure there are people out there doing this, if they are, I haven't really heard much about it. So approaching them with a deal like this may intrigue as it's not a method you see too often.

After building trust, send them your offer and what you plan to promote, see if they would be willing to give you a recommendation.

Personal recommendations from the list owner will send your profits skyrocketing. Starting with thank you pages today will eventually turn into regular, ongoing joint venture deals tomorrow.

Treat the contacts you make like pure gold.

With a little time when you become a whizz revamping your old resell products as well as creating your own products from scratch you can move towards creating your own affiliate program and have others promote your programs for you. You will want to join up to Clickbank and Paydot.com but only do it after you have more experience with and success with your own products and you're ready to take your business to the next level.

Eventually you should be building your own long term business by building a customer list, this is where www.Aweber.com comes into play. Not only will you be able to keep in regular touch with your clients but you will be able to build a long term relationship of trust with them.

How to set up your Aweber optin box:

http://www.youtube.com/watch?v=WkGZIkxGfsw

Conclusion

Congratulations for going the distance. These really are life altering skills you're developing for the rest of your life. These are the skills that will set you on the path to financial independence and once you get the hang of this you will be able to create any kind of product and market it successfully.

You are armed with the knowledge to make an income for the rest of your life. If you're looking for a quick fix get rich quick program I'm sorry to burst your bubble, this is not it. They don't exist. Behind every successful money making system you see floating around on the net is a lot of research and hard work.

That's the only way it works but at least you know for yourself that it does work. This has the power to change if you just apply it.

So just to recap, with everything you and I have gone through there's no one stand alone method to make your internet riches with, no particular method is an island unto itself, the more techniques you apply, the greater the results you'll experience. It's a fact of life, you get out what you put in.

You can revive, resuscitate and repair old resell products, the trick is to think outside of the box and I hope I've given you enough ideas to get you started.

Don't let this information overwhelm you. I've given you lots of traffic generating techniques and I don't want you to get startled into taking no action at all. These all work but only if you do them. If you pick just one to start with and to master you're well on your way. Once you get good at say the blogging then move on to Twitter. Don't try to be all things to all people because multitasking often reduces productivity. It's best to focus and get really good at one thing than it is to be a jack of all trades and a master of none.

So pick one and focus and get good at that then move on to the next technique and get good at that.

I know it seems like a lot of information but this is the real way of making money that really works. If you go back to the start and follow each step systematically and take action then success is within your grasp. At the end of the day the only thing separating the haves from the have not's is taking action. That's it.

I know you can do it, seriously once you master these steps you are acquiring a very real skill that people pay good money for, to finally demystify and figure out how to make money on the net. This is it, curtain pulled aside, you've learned everything from the grass roots up from starting with nothing to making money with your business.

The secret to making money online is that there is no secret, it's applying what you learn from others that have done it.

Now apply it.

"You can do it."
Rob Schneider from the movie "The Waterboy."

How to Create an Aweber Re-direct or "Thank You" Page

So, you want to find out how you can simply and quickly create a custom auto responder redirect page using Aweber?

Most people don't realize how powerful the redirect option really is. Utilizing Aweber's redirect feature can increase your sales immediately by up to 3 times! There are plenty of marketers out there today who still aren't utilizing this function properly.

What Is An Aweber Redirect/Thank You Page?

How many times do you sign up for a newsletter and you get immediately redirected to another page that thanks you for subscribing, and to check your inbox for your confirmation email?

In case you didn't know it, you just experienced the auto responder redirect page.

What a lot of people forget is that this is a prime piece of "web" real estate and for the most part, goes to waste with the usual default message that automatically gets sent out when someone subscribes your newsletter.

Gaining subscribers requires a certain amount of effort whether it is through paid advertising or through invested time, everything has a price so you want to make the most of every opportunity for exposure right from the start. The Aweber redirect page is the perfect way to do this.

So don't just waste your prime piece of "web" real estate. After people have joined your newsletter you've already got their interest, capitalize on that, take it to the next level and direct them to a quality offer by way of an OTO page or "One Time Offer page" or a page offering useful products that might be of interest.

So let's get started!

What You Will Need:

1. I'm assuming at this point you would already have your domain name registered and web hosting with the provider of your choice

2. A squeeze page for your subscribers to opt in to your newsletter

3. An OTO "One Time Offer" page, an up sell page or a custom made "Thank You" page offering a quality download gift as a "thanks" for joining.

4. An Aweber auto responder account, if you don't have one, you can grab one here: www.Aweber.com

Your squeeze page will have information about what you're offering full of benefit rich bullet points highlighting what they'll get joining your newsletter. You might also want to offer a quality free ebook download as an extra bonus for subscribing.

Your OTO page should thank them for joining and instruct them to check their email inbox for their confirmation email from you, immediately under it should be compelling, attention grabbing ad copy selling them on your first product.

Make sure it's a product related to what they've signed up for. It wouldn't make sense to be offering your subscribers an ebook on Horse Grooming if you're newsletter is about PLR "Private Rights Label" products unless of course the Horse Grooming ebook comes as a PLR product that your subscribers can alter and sell for profits.

So make your offer relevant!

Let's say in this instance that your newsletter or ezine is about PLR "Private Rights Label" and your domain name is www.hotPLRproducts.com to reflect this.

Let's assign:

www.hotPLRproducts.com to be the address of your squeeze page, and

http://bestofthebunch.hotPLRproducts.com to be the address of your OTO page.

You don't need to FTP your web site until the end once you've added your web form code to your squeeze page.

So you've got your squeeze page and your OTO page ready. You've finished creating it on your favorite HTML editor (Dreamweaver, FrontPage, Mozilla, etc.) and you're good to go.

Creating You Aweber Autoresponder Redirect Page

Next, log into your Aweber account.

Find "Managing List" on the left hand side of the screen.
Click "Add New".

Click "Create List"

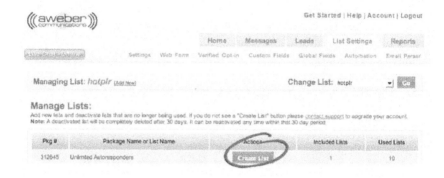

Notice you already have a "default" list name in place, this changes once you assign it a name.

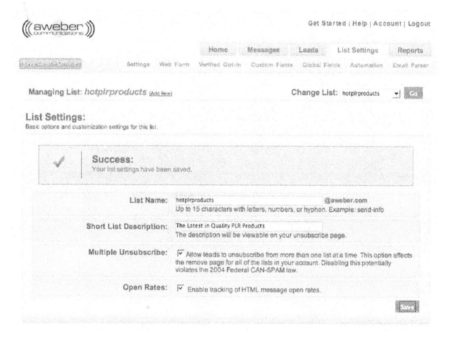

List Name – enter a name relevant to your business or newsletter content. Again, expanding on the PLR product theme, we'll call this list "hotplrproducts".

Short List Description – expands on your list name. Gives an idea of what your newsletter is about.

Multiple Unsubscribe Page – if you have multiple lists with the same recurring email addresses, once that person unsubscribes from any of your lists, they are then simultaneously removed from all of your lists.

Open Rates – this is to allow open rate tracking (keep this box checked). Handy for testing which subject lines pulled the best.

Company Branding:
Enter company information to brand various subscriber pages such as the unsubscribe link and verified opt-in confirmation pages

Company Name:	Hot PLR Products
	Example: ABC Company, Inc.
Logo URL:	
	Example: http://www.abc-company.com/logo.gif
Website URL:	http://www.hotPLRproducts.com
	Example: http://www.abc-company.com
Divider HTML Color:	

Preview unsubscribe page formatting.

[Save]

Reply Address:
Provide a valid visible "From" address that is checked regularly for sent email campaigns and receive notifications when new subscribers join your list.

Email Address	Name	From/Reply	Notifications	
charann@hotplrproducts.com	Charann	☐	☐	Add

[Save]

AWeber Communications, Inc.   Get Started | Help | Account | Logout

Company Name – Add a name that best reflects your business/content.

Logo URL – optional.

Website URL – this should be the URL of your "squeeze page"

Divider HTML Color – optional

Reply Address – the address you want your subscribers to reach you at, is also the address that will be visible when subscribers receive your emails. Include your "Email Address", along with your "Name", and check the "From/Reply" box. Make absolutely sure this is the address you want your subscribers to have access to.

You can also check the "Notifications" box if you would like to receive notification to this email address once someone joins your list.

Click "Save".

Creating Your Own Autoresponder Webform

Next, click on the "List Settings" tab.
Click on "Web Form"

Click on "Create Web Form"

Name – Describes your list

Type – I always use the "In-line" variety of web form as I like to guide subscribers to my opt-in box after they've read the benefits of joining my newsletter.

Thank You Page - now this is the clincher, this is the magic that makes the whole thing happen. This is the box that joins your squeeze page and OTO page together. If someone joins through your squeeze page, this is the box that allows your subscriber to be directed immediately to your OTO page.

Although the default code already in your "Thank You Page" box does the job, in my opinion is a waste of some valuable web real estate, you've gone to the effort to attract eyeballs to your site, the last thing you want to do is pass up a great opportunity to thank them with a gift or offer them an up sell with your OTO page.

In the "Thank You" box add your OTO/Thank You Page URL, in our case that will be http://bestofthebunch.hotPLRproducts.com

DO NOT add your main domain name as this will redirect your subscribers to the site they just left, your main site.

Open in new – optional, checking it will open your OTO page in a new window, leaving it unchecked will simply replace your squeeze page with your OTO page.

Forward Variables – for if you want to flex your JavaScript programming muscles and really customize your OTO or thank you page. Personally, the "Thank You Page" box is all we really need as it does relatively the same thing.

Already Subscribed Page – this defaults to an existing generic page from Aweber letting your subscribers know they have already signed up to the same list with the same email address.

Ad Tracking – Great for tracking exactly where your subscribers came from, especially if you have several forms of advertising campaigns running from different sources.

Start on Message – "Default" setting sends out a generic message from Aweber which you should personalize to welcome your new subscribers to your list.

Clicking "Next" will take you to the "Web Form Edit" window.

Creating Your Webform

Include the field you need.

If your line of business requires phone contact with your prospects then you custom create a "Phone Number" field.

If you would like to post your subscribers promotional material, add an "Address" field.

In this case, we'll only be asking for our subscriber's name (so that we can personalize their email) and their email address.

Click the Name field, a green plus (+) sign will open up, clicking this will then add it to the preview box on the right hand side of the screen.

Click "Save", this takes you to the next page.

How To Dress Up A Plain Old Opt-In Box

Before we get our web form code to paste into our web page, first things first.

Although you can completely bypass this stage and copy and paste your web form code directly into your WYSIWYG (What You See Is What You Get) HTML editor, I don't want you to settle for just any old plain lookin' opt-in box:

Before

Sign up for our Free 7 Day Mini Course

☑ YES!
I Want To Learn How I Can Make A
Fortune In PLR Products, Send Me
The Free E-Course

Email:

Name:

[Submit]

* Please use your **primary email address**. I have found that with free email accounts such as Hotmail and Yahoo, often legitimate and requested emails get blocked or never delivered.

I will **NEVER** sell, rent or share your email address.
That's more than a policy. **it's my personal guarantee!**

After

Sign up for our Free 7 Day Mini Course

☑ YES!
I Want To Learn How I Can Make A Fortune In
PLR Products, Send Me The Free E-Course

Email: [_____]

Name: [_____]

[Submit]

* Please use your **primary email address**. I have found that with free email
accounts such as Hotmail and Yahoo, often legitimate and requested emails get blocked or never
delivered.

I will NEVER sell, rent or share your email address.
That's more than a policy, **it's my personal guarantee!**

So tell me, which do you prefer?

Because Aweber doesn't provide it, I want you to have you a little piece of my own code that I use in all of my squeeze page and permission marketing campaigns that will give your opt-in/redirect page box that extra pop.

Although the default opt in box that Aweber generates is fully functional and all you'll need to take subscriptions and redirect to your OTO page successfully, the extra box border provides a more professional look in my opinion.

We need to do this in 2 parts:

1. Create a fancy box border to place your opt-in box within
2. Place your opt-in box within this fancy box border

1. To create your box border, here's my custom made piece of code for you to use.

```
<table
style="border: 3px dashed ; padding: 1px 4px; background-color: rgb(255, 255, 204);
width: 470px; height: 391px;"
align="center" border="0" bordercolor="#000000" cellpadding="5"
cellspacing="1">
<tbody>
<tr>
<td valign="top">
<div style="text-align: left;"> </div>
<p style="text-align: center;"> </p>
<div style="text-align: center;"> </div>
<p align="center"><span
style="font-size: 10pt; font-family: Tahoma;"><font face="tahoma"
size="4"><b> </b></font></span></p>
<div style="text-align: left;"> </div>
<div align="center">
<center>
<p><span style="font-family: arial;"> </span><br>
</p>
</center>
</div>
<span style="font-family: arial;"> </span>Love<br>
<br>
</td>
</tr>
</tbody>
</table>
```

If you scan through this code, you'll notice that it contains the word "Love" in it.

Using the word "Love" actually serves an important purpose when pinpointing exactly where you'll need to paste your web form code.

If you have the word "Love" in your text, for example if your website is about "dating" or "relationships" then you might want to keep clicking the find button until it locates the exact piece of code you're looking for.

Simply highlight and copy it by selecting CTRL C.

Access your squeeze page on your WYSIWYG HTML editor and find the spot where you'd like your opt in box to go.

Type the word "Love" (without the parenthesis), doing so makes it easier to locate exactly where you want to place your opt-in box on your web page.

The income potential is limitless!

All you have to do is take that first step towards success and you'll be cashing huge checks in no time at all.

If you want to start making more money this year in less time, I'll show you how.

Sign up for our Free 7 Day Mini Course

* Please use your **primary email address**. I have found that with free email accounts such as Hotmail and Yahoo, often legitimate and requested emails get blocked or never delivered.

I will **NEVER** sell, rent or share your email address.
That's more than a policy, it's **my personal guarantee!**

Access your HTML source code, click (CTRL F) enter "Love" into the pop up search box, click "Find Next".

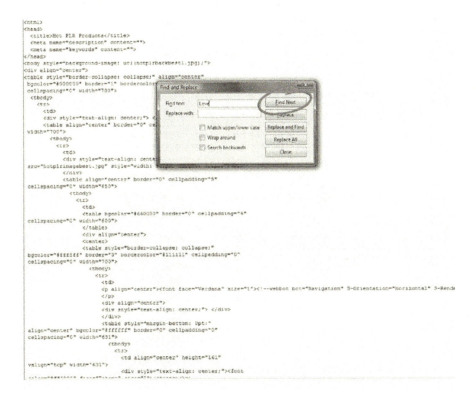

You will instantly be taken to the spot where you want to place your opt-in box border.

```
                            <br>
                     </font></font></p>
                     <div style="text-align: center;">
                     <div style="text-align: left;">
                     <div style="text-align: center;"><font
 style="font-weight: bold; background-color: rgb(255, 255, 255);"
 color="#000000" face="Arial" size="3"><font
 face="Arial, Helvetica, sans-serif" size="3">Sign up for our Free 7
Day Mini Course </font></div>
                            </div>
                            <font
 style="font-weight: bold; background-color: rgb(255, 255, 255);"
 color="#000000" face="Arial" size="3"><font
 face="Arial, Helvetica, sans-serif" size="3"><br>
                     </font></font></div>
                     <font style="font-weight: bold;" color="#000000"
 face="Arial" size="3"><font face="Arial, Helvetica, sans-serif"
 size="3"><br>
                     </font></font></div>
                     <div style="text-align: center;"><big><span
 style="font-family: arial;"><span
 style="background-color: rgb(255, 255, 0); font-weight: bold;">Love</span><br>
                     <br>
                     </span></big></div>
                     <br>
                     <div style="text-align: center;"><font
 color="#ff0000" face="Arial, Helvetica, sans-serif" size="2"><strong><font
 size="4">*</font></strong></font><font
 face="Arial, Helvetica, sans-serif" size="2"> <big>Please use your <strong>primary
email address</strong>.  I have  found that with free
email </big></font><br>
                     <font face="Arial, Helvetica, sans-serif"
 size="2"><big>accounts such as Hotmail and Yahoo, often legitimate and
requested
emails get blocked or never delivered.</big></font><br>
                     <font face="Arial, Helvetica, sans-serif"
 size="2"><big> </big></font> </div>
                     <p style="text-align: center;"><font
 face="Arial, Helvetica, sans-serif" size="2"><span
 style="font-family: arial;">I will </span><strong
 style="font-family: arial;">NEVER</strong><span
 style="font-family: arial;">
sell, rent or share your email address. <br>
That's more than a policy, </span><strong style="font-family: arial;">it's
my personal guarantee! <br>
                     </strong></font></p>
```

Delete the word "Love" then select CTRL V, this will paste your web form code in the exact spot that you want it.

```
                        <div style="text-align: center;"><font
 style="font-weight: bold; background-color: rgb(255, 255, 255);"
 color="#000000" face="Arial" size="3"><font
 face="Arial, Helvetica, sans-serif" size="3"><br>
Sign up for our Free 7
Day Mini Course <br>
                        <br>
                        </font></font> </div>
                        </div>
                        <font style="font-weight: bold;" color="#000000"
 face="Arial" size="3"><font face="Arial, Helvetica, sans-serif"
 size="3"><span style="background-color: rgb(255, 255, 0);">
                        <center><br>
                        </center>
<table
[illegible]
<tbody>
<tr>
<td valign="top">
<div style="text-align: left;"> </div>
<p style="text-align: center;"> </p>
<div style="text-align: center;"> </div>
<p align="center"><span
[illegible]
[illegible]
<div style="text-align: left;"> </div>
<div align="center">
<center>
[illegible]
</p>
</center>
</div>
[illegible]
<br>
</td>
</tr>
</tbody>
</table>
</span><br>
                        </font></font></div>
                        <br>
                        <br>
                        <div style="text-align: center;"><font
 color="#ff0000" face="Arial, Helvetica, sans-serif" size="2"><strong><font
 size="4">*</font></strong></font><font
 face="Arial, Helvetica, sans-serif" size="2"> <big>Please use your <strong>primary
email address</strong>.  I have  found that with free
email </big></font><br>
                        <font face="Arial, Helvetica, sans-serif"
 size="2"><big>accounts such as Hotmail and Yahoo, often legitimate and
requested
```

"Save".

Your box border should be in the position you want it with the word "Love" inside of it.

Sign up for our Free 7 Day Mini Course

Love

* Please use your **primary email address** I have found that with free email

2. You're almost there, now we're going to place our Aweber web form code within that box, this is the code that redirects to your OTO page.

Where To Place Your Webform Code

Access Aweber.

Go to List Settings, then select "Web Form".

Click "Get HTML", this is the magical code you'll be adding to the HTML code in your squeeze page which will redirect it to your OTO page.

To highlight the code to copy, click within the window, select CTRL A (Select All), then CTRL C (Copy), you now have your web form HTML code ready to paste into your squeeze page.

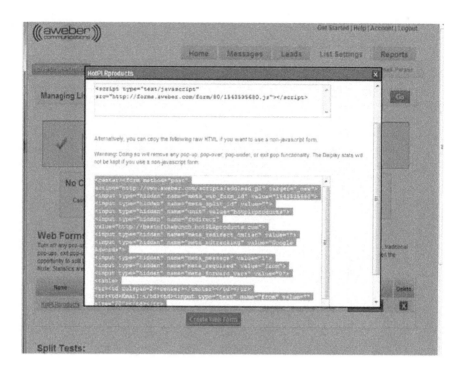

Go back to your squeeze page HTML source code, now for the cool part, search for "Love" again by selecting CTRL F (Find) in the search pop up box, click "Find Next".

```html
<html>
<head>
  <title>Hot PLR Products</title>
  <meta name="description" content="">
  <meta name="keywords" content="">
</head>
<body style="background-image: url(hotplrbackbest1.jpg);">
<div align="center">
<table style="border-collapse: collapse;" align="center"
 bgcolor="#000000" border="1" bordercolor
 cellspacing="0" width="700">
  <tbody>
    <tr>
      <td>
      <div style="text-align: center;"> <
      <table align="center" border="0" ce
 width="700">
        <tbody>
          <tr>
            <td>
            <div style="text-align: cente
 src="hotplrimagebest.jpg" style="width:
            </div>
            <table align="center" border="0" cellpadding="5"
 cellspacing="0" width="650">
              <tbody>
                <tr>
                  <td>
                  <table bgcolor="#660000" border="0" cellpadding="4"
 cellspacing="0" width="600">
                  </table>
                  <div align="center">
                  <center>
                  <table style="border-collapse: collapse;"
 bgcolor="#ffffff" border="3" bordercolor="#111111" cellpadding="0"
 cellspacing="0" width="700">
                    <tbody>
                      <tr>
                        <td>
                        <p align="center"><font face="Verdana" size="1"><!--webbot bot="Navigation" S-Orientation
                        </p>
                        <div align="center">
                        <div style="text-align: center;"> </div>
                        </div>
                        <table style="margin-bottom: 0pt;"
```

```html
face="Arial" size="3"><font face="Arial, Helvetica, sans-serif"
size="3"><span style="background-color: rgb(255, 255, 0);">
                        <center><br>
                        </center>
                        <table
style="border: 3px dashed ; padding: 1px 4px; background-color: rgb(255, 255, 204); width: 470px;
align="center" border="0" bordercolor="#000000" cellpadding="5"
cellspacing="1">
                          <tbody>
                            <tr>
                              <td valign="top">
                              <div style="text-align: left;"> </div>
                              <p style="text-align: center;"> </p>
                              <div style="text-align: center;"> </div>
                              <p align="center"><span
style="font-size: 10pt; font-family: Tahoma;"><font face="tahoma"
size="4"><b> </b></font></span></p>
                              <div style="text-align: left;"> </div>
                              <div align="center">
                              <center>
                              <p><span style="font-family: arial;"></span><br>
                              </p>
                              </center>
                              </div>
                              <span style="font-family: arial;"></span>Love<br>
                              <br>
                              </td>
                            </tr>
                          </tbody>
                        </table>
                      </span><br>
                      </font></font></div>
                      <br>
                      <br>
                      <div style="text-align: center;"><font
color="#ff0000" face="Arial, Helvetica, sans-serif" size="2"><strong><font
size="4">*</font></strong></font><font
face="Arial, Helvetica, sans-serif" size="2"> <big>Please use your <strong>primary
```

You will be taken to where your box border is, delete the word "Love" and in its place, select CTRL V, this pastes your web form/redirect code.

```
color="#000000" face="Arial" size="3"><font
face="Arial, Helvetica, sans-serif" size="3">Sign up for our Free 7
Day Mini Course <br>
                <br>
                </font></font> </div>
            </div>
            <font style="font-weight: bold;" color="#000000"
face="Arial" size="2"><font face="Arial, Helvetica, sans-serif"
size="3"><span style="background-color: rgb(255, 255, 0);">
                <center><br>
                </center>
                <table
style="border: 3px dashed ; padding: 1px 4px; background-color: rgb(255, 255, 204); width: 470px; height: 391px;
align="center" border="0" bordercolor="#000000" cellpadding="5"
cellspacing="1">
                    <tbody>
                    <tr>
                    <td valign="top">
                    <div style="text-align: left;"> </div>
                    <p style="text-align: center;"> </p>
                    <div style="text-align: center;"> </div>
                    <p align="center"><span
style="font-size: 10pt; font-family: Tahoma;"><font face="tahoma"
size="4"><b> </b></font></span></p>
                    <div style="text-align: left;"> </div>
                    <div align="center">
                    <center>
                    <p><span style="font-family: arial;"></span><br>
                    </p>
                    </center>
                    </div>
                    <span style="font-family: arial;"></span>
```

"Save".

There you have your stellar opt-in/redirect URL box ready to go.

If you want to start making more money this year in less time, I'll show you how.

Sign up for our Free 7 Day Mini Course

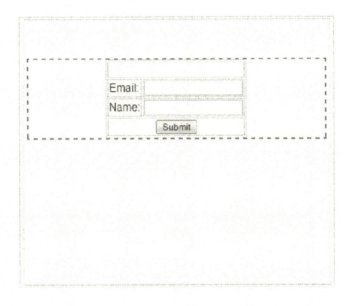

The box may appear a little too long or wide, just use the arrows in each of the corners to resize it the way you like.

You can also add text to help your opt in box jump out at your potential subscribers.

Don't forget to select "Browse" or "Preview", depending upon which editor you're using, this previews how your site will appear online.

Sign up for our Free 7 Day Mini Course

☑ YES!
I Want To Learn How I Can Make A Fortune In PLR
Products, Send Me The Free E-Course

Email: [   ]
Name: [   ]
[Submit]

* Please use your **primary email address**. I have found that with free email accounts such as Hotmail and Yahoo, often legitimate and requested emails get blocked or r delivered.

I will **NEVER** sell, rent or share your email address.
That's more than a policy, **it's my personal guarantee!**

All that's left to do is to FTP your squeeze page and OTO page.

Testing

After FTP'ing (File Transfer Protocol) your web files, your site should now be live on the internet. Just type in your squeeze page URL into your favorite web browser and it should pop up.

Run a quick test to see how your redirect page works. Enter your name and email address into your opt in box, click on the "Submit" button and you should be immediately redirected to your awesome OTO page.

Don't forget you need to tap into a payment system in order to take payments and you're done. If you don't already have a PayPal account, you can grab one for free here at www.Paypal.com

So just add yourself a Paypal payment button to your OTO page, set the amount you'd like to charge for your product offer and start taking orders today!

Congratulations!

You now know how to create your own thank you pages and you can start taking advantage of this prime piece of virtual real estate.

What Next?

Thank-you for reading. As promised, below are the details for your bonus Resell Rights Profits membership.

Here's the special URL you will need to goto to sign up:

http://resell-rights-profits.com/go/signup_jv.php

Here is the password you will need to enter to activate your full Gold membership for my Resell Rights Profits membership site:

abrakadabra

The regular price of your Resell Rights Profits membership is up to $97 per month, but as a valued reader - you get a FULL membership for free. You pay nothing - ever.

We're adding fresh new content every month, so please take advantage of this amazing offer and propel your internet business to the next level.

Don't forget as a member of http://www.resell-rights-profits.com you also become an affiliate, and make 50% recurring for each and every member you refer. Click on 'Earn Money', and 'Promo Tools' in the members area to find out more.

To your success!

Leigh Burke.

Index

www.ingramcontent.com/pod-product-compliance
Lightning Source LLC
Chambersburg PA
CBHW051233050326
40689CB00007B/912